Looking at
SETTLEMENTS

Judith Anderson

W
FRANKLIN WATTS
LONDON·SYDNEY

First published in 2006 by

Franklin Watts

338 Euston Road

London NW1 3BH

Franklin Watts Australia

Hachette Children's Books

Level 17/207 Kent Street

Sydney NSW 2000

Editor: Jennifer Schofield

Consultant: Steve Watts

(FRGS, Principal Lecturer University of Sunderland)

Art director: Jonathan Hair

Design: Mo Choy

Artwork: Ian Thompson

Picture researcher: Kathy Lockley

Acknowledgements:

©Walter Bibikow/Image Bank/Getty Images 17. ©Bildarchiv Mondheim GmbH/Alamy Images 27.
©Martin Bond/Still Pictures 42. ©Fridmar Damm/ZEFA/Corbis 22. ©Mark Edwards/Still Pictures 20, 35t. ©Eye Ubiquitous/
Hutchison 6, 9, 34. © Kevin Fleming/Corbis 16. © Tim Graham/Corbis 40. ©Sally & Richard Greenhill 13, 43.
©Robert Harding Picture Library 14, 15, 30, 31, 35b.©Peter Horree/Alamy Images 41. ©Houghton/TopFoto.co.uk 8.
©Richard I'Anson/Lonely Planet Images 3b, 11, 33t, Cover. © Janet Jarman/Corbis 21. ©Peter Kingsford/TopFoto.co.uk 23.
©Jean-Pierre Lescouret/Corbis 26. ©Kate Lockley 19b. ©NASA/Science Photo Library 29. ©Pacific Press Service/Alamy Images 33b.
©Powered by Light/Alan Spencer/Alamy Images 28. ©Hartmut Schwarzbach/Still Pictures 38. © Dennis Scott/Corbis 3t, 4/5,
44/5, 46/7, Cover. ©Jochen Tack/Still Pictures 19t. ©Charlotte Thege/Still Pictures 39. ©TopFoto.co.uk 10. ©Ullstein-Eckel/
Still Pictures 36. ©Patrick Ward/Alamy Images 24. © Alison Wright/Corbis 25.

Every attempt has been made to clear copyright.

Should there be any inadvertent omission please

apply to the publisher for rectification.

A CIP catalogue record for this book

is available from the British Library.

ISBN 10: 0 7496 6782 6

ISBN 13: 978 0 7496 6782 5

Dewey Classification: 307

Printed in China

Franklin Watts is a division of Hachette Children's Books.

Contents

What is a settlement?

Asettlement is a place where people live. Settlements can be any size, and they are found all over the world. A small cluster of fishermen's huts is a settlement. So is a city with a population of several million people.

URBAN SETTLEMENTS

Towns and cities are urban settlements. A town usually has a population of between 1,000 and 100,000 people. It has homes, shops, schools, and places of work such as factories and offices. A city usually has a population of more than 100,000 people. It may have a cathedral or mosque, government offices and a university as well as homes, shops, schools and workplaces.

Lagos in Nigeria is one of the world's fastest-growing cities.

RURAL SETTLEMENTS

Settlements in the countryside are called rural settlements. They are small, and range in size from an isolated farm to a few hundred homes in a village. A village may have other buildings and services such as a church, shops and a school. However, very small villages, or hamlets, are usually no bigger than a handful of homes and farms.

TYPES OF VILLAGES

Look at the sketch maps of the two different settlements below. Village A is stretched out, almost in a line along the main road that runs through it. This type of settlement is called a linear village. Village B is clustered around a crossroads. It is called a nucleated village.

Study a map of your area and try to identify linear and nucleated villages near you. Why do you think many villages are shaped like this?

LAND USE

The land in and around settlements is used in a variety of ways. Housing, factories, parks and farmland are all different types of land use. What other types of land use can you think of?

You are going to draw a sketch map of a settlement near you. First, draw the main features such as roads, rivers and important buildings. Then use different colours to shade in different types of land use. Remember to include a key. Which type of land use covers the biggest area? Why do you think this is?

Village A

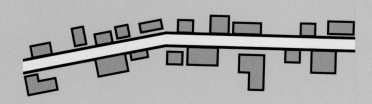

Village B

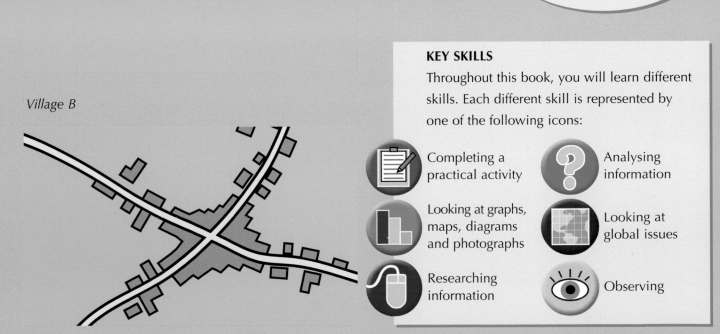

HELPING HAND
Throughout this book, this helping hand will give you useful tips and hints.

KEY SKILLS
Throughout this book, you will learn different skills. Each different skill is represented by one of the following icons:

Completing a practical activity

Analysing information

Looking at graphs, maps, diagrams and photographs

Looking at global issues

Researching information

Observing

How settlements began

Many settlements are very old, and began because people needed to live near each other, in family groups, for protection and in order to farm and trade together.

THE START OF A SETTLEMENT

Look at the two photographs of settlements on these pages. Why do you think people first settled in each place? Think about different needs the settlers may have had: water, good farmland, shelter, defence, transport, trade and raw materials. Make a table like the one below, filling in the "reasons" column.

SETTLEMENT	REASONS FOR DEVELOPMENT
Inverness, Scotland	
Mining town, Zimbabwe	

One thing all settlements need is a supply of fresh water. Nowadays water can be pumped from a lake or reservoir some distance away. However, in the past, people had to live near a water source.

The River Ness flows through the town of Inverness in Scotland.

RIVERS AND ROADS

If you follow the course of a river on a map, you will almost certainly find villages and towns clustered along its banks. This is because not only did rivers provide water for drinking and farming, but they also provided the main means of transport and trade between settlements. Many of the world's great cities such as Cairo in Egypt, Vienna in Austria and New York in the USA grew up on the banks of large rivers.

Other settlements began at a crossing of some sort – either of a river or at a crossroads. Many market towns began in this way because the crossing was a natural place for people to meet and trade.

OTHER NATURAL FEATURES

Farming settlements depend on rich soil for crops or good grazing land, while coastal fishing settlements cluster around bays.

Some settlements depend on other natural resources such as forests or underground mineral deposits. Others were built on hilltops or in the bends of rivers for defence against attack. What else may have influenced the site of a particular settlement? What other natural features can you think of?

Of course, many settlements have changed in purpose and scope over the years, and not all settlements are old. Nowadays many people do not work on the land around their settlement, and they do not depend on a river for trade. Yet discovering how our settlements began can help us understand how they change and develop over time.

How can you find out about the origins of the settlement where you live?

This picture of a gold mine in Zimbabwe shows a housing settlement in the foreground.

HELPING HAND
The Internet, your local tourist office, local maps and old photographs will provide useful information on your settlement.

Changes over time

Old settlements rarely meet modern needs. As populations grow, they need bigger transport networks, a wider variety of businesses, changing industries and a greater emphasis on leisure activities than ever before. So how do settlements adapt?

This is Sydney Harbour in Australia in the 1920s.

GROWTH

Growth is one of the main ways in which many settlements have changed over time. A growing population needs more homes and workplaces. There are now more and larger settlements than at any time in the past.

LAND USE

Growth is not the only change. Developing industry and technology, changing farming methods, new methods of transport and better communications networks have all had a huge impact on settlements and how land is used. A housing estate may be built on farmland or a warehouse turned into offices. A fishing village may become a tourist attraction.

Find out about an area of land where you live that has recently changed in use or purpose. Do you think the change is for the better?

Look at the two aerial photographs of Sydney Harbour in Australia.

What differences can you see between the two photographs? Describe the changes that have taken place. Do you think these changes are successful? What disadvantages can you think of?

HELPING HAND
Always try to consider the environmental, economic and social impact of change. Who are the winners and who are the losers?

DECLINE

Not all change is about regeneration and growth. Sometimes, a settlement cannot adapt to changes. This is particularly the case for settlements that have depended on a natural resource such as timber, coal or fish. When the resource is used up or no longer required, people may lose their jobs and move away in search of new work.

Sydney Harbour today.

KEY SKILLS

 Interpreting aerial photographs

 Analysing information

 Making comparisons; understanding change

You are going to look at changes over time in a settlement near you. First, try to find out about the origins of your settlement. Use old photographs, maps and written descriptions to find out as much as you can. Are any of the original buildings still there? Have they changed in use, or have they been knocked down and replaced by something else? Has your settlement grown, or declined in the last 50 years? Why do you think this is?

11

Where you live

What is it like where you live? Is your home in a village, or a town or a city? Find out why you live there. Do you like it? Is there anything you want to change about your settlement?

KEY SKILLS

Making a poster; carrying out a survey

Interpreting the survey results

Displaying results as a bar graph

Using the Internet and newspapers to do research

MAKING A POSTER

You are going to make a poster about where you live. Start by introducing your settlement with a brief description, giving factual information such as its population size and location. Is it in the north, south, east or west of the country? A map will provide you with an exact reference. Would you describe your settlement as rural or urban?

Now, either draw a sketch map of your settlement, or attach a street map to your poster. Make sure your map shows any rivers, main roads, your school and your home.

Does your settlement have any distinguishing features such as special buildings, a big park or a shopping centre? Annotate your map with arrows and labels explaining anything you particularly like or dislike about the settlement. You could take photographs of these things.

HELPING HAND
You can find street maps on the Internet by logging on to www.streetmap.com and entering your postcode.

YOUR NEIGHBOURHOOD

Your neighbourhood is the area close to your home. If you live in a village, the whole settlement is your neighbourhood. If you live in a city, your neighbourhood is probably a smaller area, and may even have its own name. It may include local housing, a few shops, your school, and a park or play area.

LOCAL COMMUNITY

The people who live in your neighbourhood make up your local community. You are going to complete a survey to find out what your local community thinks of the neighbourhood. Do they find the buildings and environment attractive? Do they think the location of the settlement is convenient, or do they have problems with things such as local shops, transport and services?

Using the table on page 13 as a starting point, develop a questionnaire to find out what your neighbours think of where they live.

Do you know your neighbours?
Is it easy to meet people in your neighbourhood?

YOUR NEIGHBOURHOOD

IS IT:	very attractive	quite attractive	not sure	unattractive	very unattractive

IS IT:	very convenient	quite convenient	not sure	inconvenient	very inconvenient

Which answers were the most common? Display your results on bar graphs and add them to the poster you have made. Your graphs may look like this:

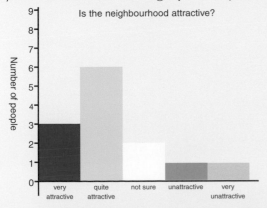

DIFFERENT OPINIONS

Sometimes people in a neighbourhood have different opinions about a local issue. It may be a new building, or it may be the best way to deal with a problem such as traffic.

A good way to investigate neighbourhood issues and views is to read the letters page of your local newspaper. You might like to cut out one or two of the letters and stick them onto the bottom of your poster.

13

Housing

Housing forms the largest part of most settlements. Smaller settlements may consist of one type of housing only, such as huts or cottages. Larger settlements usually consist of many different types, such as blocks of flats, terraced houses, bungalows or slum housing.

TYPES OF HOUSING

The types of housing people live in vary enormously from place to place. This may be due to cost, or it may be due to factors such as climate, space, the availability of different building materials, or local traditions and culture.

These coastal timber homes in Borneo are built on stilts above the water.

Some homes are simply constructed from local materials. Other homes are made from materials such as cement, brick and steel that have been manufactured elsewhere. Make a list of all the different types of housing you can think of. What are the main differences? What are the similarities?

Look carefully at the photographs of the two different types of housing shown here. Decide whether they are:

- making the most of the available space
- quick and cheap to build
- safe and secure.

Which of these requirements do you think is the most important? Discuss your answers with a friend.

These inner-city, brick-built homes in Bradford, UK, are built in straight terraces.

YOUR HOME

Take a photograph or draw a sketch of the outside of your home. Annotate your sketch or photograph with labels to show the different features. What building materials have been used? How is your home adapted for your climate?

HELPING HAND
So that your photograph is not damaged, stick it onto a piece of card and write on the card rather than on the photograph.

Perhaps your home is similar to other homes in your neighbourhood. Similar types of housing are often clustered together on urban housing estates, in rural villages or in the city suburbs. What do you think are the reasons for this?

Work

Wherever there are settlements, there is work. This may be growing food or building homes, or providing a service such as teaching or nursing. Businesses and factories create more jobs. All settlements depend on an effective working community. However, sometimes there are not enough paid jobs for everyone.

A SPECIFIC INDUSTRY

Some settlements rely on a particular industry to provide most of the jobs for people in the local community. Farming settlements, fishing villages, mining towns and holiday resorts are all examples of this. However, while larger settlements may have their origins in a particular type of work, most expand to include many different businesses, public services and industries, all employing people in a wide variety of jobs.

Stacking timber at a sawmill in Piercetown, Arkansas, USA. Some settlements like Piercetown depend almost entirely on the timber industry.

JOBS SURVEY

What are the different types of work in your settlement? Carry out a survey of as many adults as you can, asking them what jobs they do. Then sort the answers into groups and display the information on a bar graph, like the one here. You may want to add other types of work to the ones shown.

In the past, people tended to live close to their place of work, but nowadays they often travel several kilometres and sometimes commute to work in a different settlement entirely. How far do the people in your survey travel to work each day? What effect might this have on the settlement?

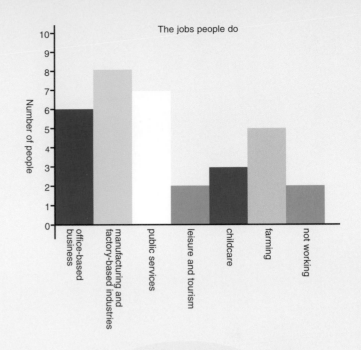

The jobs people do

(Bar graph – x-axis: office-based business, manufacturing and factory-based industries, public services, leisure and tourism, childcare, farming, not working; y-axis: Number of people)

HELPING HAND
Teachers, nurses, local council employees and the police all work in public services.

HITEC City in Hyderabad, India.

NEW SITES

Today, workplaces are often situated on industrial estates at the edges of settlements. This is usually because there is more space for new buildings, costs are lower and main roads between settlements are close by.

Look at this photograph of the Hyderabad Information Technology Engineering Consultancy City (HITEC City) in Hyderabad, India.

The office park was built to house India's top information technology businesses. The site covers 20km². In 2004 it contained over 50 different companies, employing around 20,000 people. It is predicted that by 2008 there will be over 75,000 people working and living in HITEC City. Find HITEC City on a map. Look at the surrounding areas. Do you think this is a good development for local people? What are the disadvantages of the development?

Shops

Shops are a vital part of most settlements. We rely on them for food, clothing, household goods – almost everything we need. Many of our towns and villages have their origins in the weekly market that brought people in from the countryside to buy and sell produce. However, shops and shopping habits have changed a great deal over time.

TYPES OF SHOP

Shops vary in size and type from market stalls to local shops, high street stores, supermarkets or out of town shopping centres. Yet items such as apples, bread or a newspaper can be bought at all these different types of shop. So how do we decide where we want to do our shopping?

You are going to investigate where you and your family shop during the course of a month, and why you go there. First, make a list of all the different places you go to shop, and the things you buy there. Then make a note of why you chose that particular shopping location. It may be useful to put your data in a table like the one below.

On a local map, mark your home and the different places where you shopped.

Do you think there is a good range of different shops where you live? How far did you have to travel to reach some of them? Which is the furthest? What did you buy there? Do you think it was worth travelling the distance?

Type of shop	Number of times	What for?	Why?
Market			
Local store			
High street store			
Supermarket			
Out of town shopping mall			

HELPING HAND
When measuring the distance of each journey, be sure to follow your exact route.

KEY SKILLS

Carrying out
a survey

Annotating a map
and measuring
distances

Interpreting
information

Shopping centre in Oberhausen in Germany.

CHANGING TIMES

Many smaller shops and specialist stores
(selling one type of goods only, such as shoes)
are disappearing from our local communities
because of competition from big stores and out
of town shopping centres. Does this matter?
What impact does it have on local communities?

Some people prefer to shop on the Internet,
without leaving home at all. This is especially
true for more expensive items, such as holidays,
or electrical goods. The Internet is having a
direct impact on many high streets as shops
such as travel agents struggle to keep pace
with changing shopping habits.

*People are increasingly choosing to book holidays via
the Internet rather than through traditional travel agents.*

19

Water

Water, along with food and shelter, is a basic requirement for life in a settlement. We all need it for drinking, cooking and washing. Rural settlements depend on water for healthy livestock and watering crops. It is also an essential part of many industrial processes in our towns and cities.

AVAILABILITY OF WATER

Many of us can use as much water as we want, simply by turning on a tap. This water comes from a water purification plant where it is filtered and disinfected before it is piped into our homes. However in some parts of the world water is not so readily available. This may be due to low rainfall, or because people cannot afford to dig wells, lay pipes or build pumps.

School children walk past untreated sewage water in Port-au-Prince, Haiti.

Some people rely on unpurified water from an open well or a local river, which may carry water-borne organisms. These can cause illnesses, such as dysentery, which kill thousands of people every year.

DROUGHT

Low rainfall, or drought, is a particular problem for many less economically developed countries (LEDCs). Many LEDCs do not have sufficient pipes, reservoirs and tanks for storing and delivering water to areas that need it. Even when it does rain – during the monsoon season, for example – the water does not have time to soak into the earth and replenish the wells and aquifers below the ground.

DIFFERENT SOLUTIONS

There are a number of ways to deal with drought, from building more and deeper wells, to constructing huge dams along rivers to store water and irrigate farmland.

You are going to look at how people in India try to overcome the problems of drought.

First, use an atlas to find a physical map and rainfall chart of India. Locate features such as desert and areas affected by monsoon rains. Next, use the Internet to research the construction of dams along the Narmada River, and new tube wells in the area. What are the advantages and disadvantages of each method?

A VILLAGE IN INDIA

Villages in Rajasthan in India frequently experience severe drought. However, instead of building dams and wells, some villages are choosing instead to concentrate on reviving traditional methods of "water harvesting". Such methods ensure that when rain falls, it remains in the soil.

In Laporiya, villagers have built a system of embankments around rectangular plots of land. The embankments help the soil to retain the rain, watering crops and also draining the water deep below the surface where it can seep back into the aquifers or collect in storage tanks for use during the rest of the year. Write a short report weighing up the advantages and disadvantages of dams, new wells and traditional water harvesting. What do you think should be done about the problem of drought in India?

These women in Laporiya are tending their crop. Embankments have raised water levels in the wells and increased crop yield by up to 12 times.

HELPING HAND
Try to consider the environment, cost, long-term effectiveness and the impact on local communities.

Transport

Almost every person in a settlement depends on transport of one type or another. How do you get to school? How do your parents travel to work? How do farms and businesses transport goods and materials? Bicycles, cars, buses, trucks, trains, ships and planes provide the vital links between home, school, workplace, farm and factory.

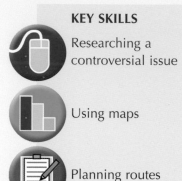

KEY SKILLS

Researching a controversial issue

Using maps

Planning routes

Trucks transport goods thousands of kilometres across Canada.

NEGATIVE IMPACT

The variety and speed of modern forms of transport mean that we can all travel further and transport things to more places than ever before. However, any increase in the volume of transport has other, less welcome, effects. Air and noise pollution, traffic jams, damage to the environment, speeding and car parking all create huge problems in our towns and cities.

CONGESTION CHARGING

London is the capital city of the United Kingdom. Like many large cities, the volume of traffic has increased significantly in recent years, causing pollution, congestion, journey delays and parking problems. To solve these problems, London's mayor introduced a congestion charge in 2003. The charge is paid by all private cars and trucks entering a "congestion zone" in the centre of the city during daytime hours. The idea behind the congestion charge is to reduce the volume of traffic by encouraging people to use other methods of transport such as bicycles, buses and trains.

People who travel by bus in central London do not pay the congestion charge.

DOES IT WORK?

Some people were worried about the congestion charge. They thought it might be bad for the small businesses and shops in central London as deliveries would cost more and customers might stay away. Others feared that there might not be enough buses and trains to cope with the extra passengers.

Nevertheless, the average journey time within the congestion zone has been cut by 15 per cent, and the volume of traffic was initially reduced by about 18 per cent.

See what you can find out about the congestion charge. Do you think it is a successful way to deal with traffic? What other ways can you think of to reduce congestion?

PLAN YOUR ROUTE

Find a map of central London. Plan a route by car, bus and train for these journeys:

- Hyde Park to the Barbican
- Euston Station to London Bridge Station
- Waterloo Bridge to Pimlico.

Remember to include any walking you may need to do.

HELPING HAND
Log on to www.tfl.gov.uk/tfl/maps-home.shtml for different transport maps of London.

Public services

Public services are services that are provided by a government for the benefit of the community. They are paid for with money collected from taxes and may include hospitals, schools, libraries, fire stations, the police, waste disposal and recycling centres.

RURAL AND URBAN PUBLIC SERVICES

Large towns and cities usually have all of these services, but smaller rural settlements do not. A village might have a small cottage hospital or a primary school, but often residents have to travel to a larger settlement to have an operation, attend college, or visit a public library.

One way for smaller, more isolated settlements to get around this problem is to have public services brought to them. Mobile libraries and travelling health clinics are good examples of this. However, sometimes these services are closed down because it is more cost-effective to develop bigger hospitals, schools and libraries in densely populated urban areas.

The Australian Flying Doctor Service provides medical assistance for people in some of Australia's most remote and isolated settlements.

DIVIDED OPINIONS

Imagine that a small village school near you is threatened with closure. Government planners think it will be better for the few village children to travel to a newer, bigger school in a town five kilometres away. Some people in the village disagree. The panels on the right set out some of the arguments.

Can you think of any other arguments for and against closing the village school? Try to think about the impact on the local community, the environment, who pays and who benefits.

Should school buses like this be paid for by local government or by the people who use them?

Local school
- Part of local community
- Children can walk to school
- Everyone knows each other

New school
- Better facilities
- Bigger mix of children and teachers
- More cost-effective

SERVICES NEAR YOU

You are going to think about four public services in your area: your school; your nearest Accident and Emergency Department; a library and a police station. First, mark the location of your home and each of these four services on a local map. How far is it to each? What is the most convenient route? What is the best method of transport? Think about cost, distance, speed and convenience. Do not forget to consider parking if you choose to go by car. Do you think these services are in a good location? Have you encountered any difficulty with your journeys?

Write a letter to your local council saying how you think access to these services might be improved. Remember that local government is funded by taxpayers' money and spending must be kept within a strict budget.

KEY SKILLS

 Assessing different arguments

 Measuring distances on a map

 Writing a formal letter

HELPING HAND
Remember to use formal language when you write your letter.

Leisure

Leisure is about relaxation, sport and entertainment – the things we do in our free time. Today, many people have more free time and more money to spend on leisure activities than in the past. This has brought many changes to our towns and cities as new sports complexes, cinemas, theatres, shopping centres and tourist attractions are built to accommodate our growing leisure needs.

LEISURE ZONES

Some big cities have whole entertainment zones. These may be new areas on the outskirts of the city, with shops, restaurants, cinemas and sports facilities. Other cities may have an older entertainment zone such as the West End in central London, UK, where there are many cinemas and theatres. A few cities such as Las Vegas in the USA depend almost exclusively on the leisure industry.

KEY SKILLS

Assessing a controversial issue

Using persuasive writing

Although Las Vegas is in the Nevada Desert, millions of tourists travel there each year. Its streets are lined with casinos and hotels.

GREEN SPACES

Leisure is not just about buildings. It is also about green spaces such as parks, nature reserves and the "green belts" around many cities set up to preserve areas of countryside between different settlements. Green spaces are as much a part of our towns and cities as the buildings, roads and other structures.

INVESTIGATING LOCAL NEEDS

You are going to carry out an investigation into the leisure needs of a typical town. Look at the sketch map on the right. It shows the main residential areas, along with the existing leisure facilities of a town. There is a large area of wasteland on the southern edge of the town. Town planners must decide whether to turn it into a nature reserve with cycle paths, or allow developers to build a cinema and sports complex.

Prepare arguments for and against the two types of land use proposed for the wasteland site. Try to consider issues of cost, the environment, the local community, jobs and the impact on existing facilities. Which do you think would be most beneficial for the local community? Write a campaign leaflet putting across your point of view.

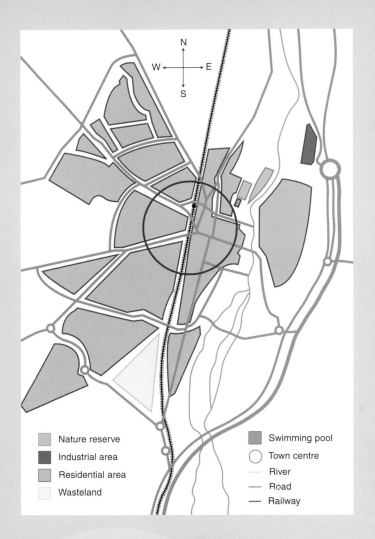

■ Nature reserve	■ Swimming pool
■ Industrial area	○ Town centre
■ Residential area	— River
■ Wasteland	— Road
	— Railway

HELPING HAND
Remember that you want to persuade people to agree with your views.

Vondelpark in the centre of Amsterdam was first laid out in the 1860s. It continues to be one of the city's most popular parks.

Links with other settlements

Very few people live in complete isolation. We depend on each other for goods, services and information. In the same way, very few settlements are entirely self-sufficient. Many villages, towns and cities have developed a complex network of interdependence, trading and exchanging skills, news, wealth, government, ideas and technology.

TRANSPORT LINKS

Look at a map of your county, region or state. The network of roads allows people and goods to travel quickly and easily from one settlement to another. Railways, rivers, airports and coastal ports provide other transport links. What settlements have you been to? Make a list, saying why you went there, and how you travelled. Display the information on a spider diagram like the one on the right. Replace the question marks with your destinations and the transport blocks with the type of transport that you used.

KEY SKILLS

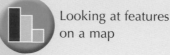
Looking at features on a map

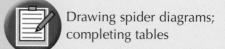
Analysing information

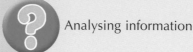
Drawing spider diagrams; completing tables

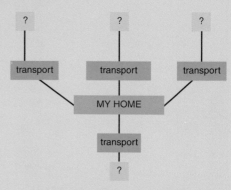

Many islands off the coast of Scotland depend on boats and helicopters to transport goods, post and people to and from the mainland.

BORDER HEATHER

TELECOMMUNICATIONS

In the past, people from different settlements exchanged information, traded and governed by travelling from place to place. Communication was slow, and weakened further by events such as war, natural disaster or bad weather. Nowadays, telecommunications such as the telephone, e-mail and the Internet as well as radio and television mean that people can communicate with each other, often instantly, over vast distances from almost anywhere in the world.

Modern telecommunications rely on satellites like this one launched by NASA.

KEEPING IN TOUCH

How do you communicate with people in other settlements? Imagine that it is your best friend's birthday. How will you send a greeting if your friend lives in your street? What if they live two kilometres away? What if they live 100 kilometres away? What if they live in another country? It may be useful to draw up a table for your answers.

HELPING HAND
There is no right or wrong answer, although you may want to take cost and speed into account.

A GLOBAL VILLAGE?

Developments in transport and telecommunications have had huge benefits for trade, industry and tourism. It is almost as if someone thousands of kilometres away is a neighbour, and we are living in a "global village". Yet many people do not have access to telephones, computers and long-distance air travel. The global village exists only for those who can afford it. Others prefer not to exploit all the global links between settlements because of damage to the environment caused by aeroplanes and cars. What do you think?

Seaside resort

The seaside is a popular holiday destination. However, tourists need more than sun, sea and sand when they arrive. They need accommodation, food, shops and leisure facilities. A seaside resort is a town that caters for seaside visitors.

BUILDINGS

Many seaside resorts began as fishing villages. Some resorts may still have an old harbour area or "old town" near the sea with narrow streets and traditional buildings. Sometimes these areas become a tourist attraction in their own right.

Most seaside resorts have hotels, restaurants and shops along the seafront so that tourists can stay and eat as close to the beaches as possible. In some resorts, a shortage of available land along the sea front has resulted in the construction of high-rise hotels to accommodate growing numbers of tourists. Some people call this "over development" because the natural attractions of the original settlement are lost.

Look at the photograph below of Benidorm in Spain. Restaurants, hotels and high-rise buildings line the beach to cater for tourists. What problems might be associated with this kind of development?

Benidorm in Spain is a very popular seaside resort. It has many hotels along the seafront.

LOCAL IMPACT

Seaside resorts create jobs, but they also push up the price of land in the most popular areas and local people may find they cannot afford to buy properties there. Natural habitats may also be damaged by all the new roads, buildings and extra pollution. Because of this, some tourists choose to visit "eco-friendly" beach resorts, where efforts are made to prevent the exploitation of both the local community and the environment.

A resort in Zanzibar, Tanzania.

HIGH AND LOW SEASONS

Some seaside resorts are popular all year round, but many have a "high" season, often during school holidays or when the climate is comfortably warm, and a "low" season when it is cooler or wet. During the low season, there is not a lot of work for local people to do and they may have to find other employment.

SEND A POSTCARD

You are going to investigate two seaside resorts – one in your own country, if possible, and a contrasting one from abroad. You will need to use maps, guidebooks and the Internet to carry out your research. Write a postcard from each place, describing the resort, its location, buildings and environment, and saying what you like and dislike.

HELPING HAND
Ask a travel agent for some brochures and travel information on your two resorts.

Capital city

KEY SKILLS

Using an atlas

Carrying out research

Looking at planning issues

Every country has a capital city. This is where the government has its main offices and makes decisions about how the country is run. The leader of the country usually lives there, as well as a large number of ordinary people.

FEATURES OF A CAPITAL CITY

Capital cities are not just centres of government. Banks, businesses and the armed forces may also have their headquarters there. There is usually a large university, important museums and places of worship such as cathedrals and mosques. Representatives of foreign governments, called diplomats, also have their embassies there.

TRANSPORT

Transport links are a vital part of any capital city. The capital's size and its importance mean that it has to be able to cope with millions of commuters and visitors, as well as all the goods and raw materials travelling in and out of the city.

LOCATION

Look at this map of France. Paris is the capital city. Motorways and railways fan out from Paris to all parts of the country and beyond. The main airport is located on the outskirts of Paris. Paris is built along the banks of France's biggest river, the Seine. Many of the world's capital cities are built alongside important rivers, or near the coast, because in the past this was the best way to trade and to travel. Other capital cities are located near the centre of the country because they are easy for most people to get to.

Some capital cities, such as Islamabad in Pakistan, are not near the centre of the country. Islamabad was built in northern Pakistan partly because it is cooler and less crowded there.

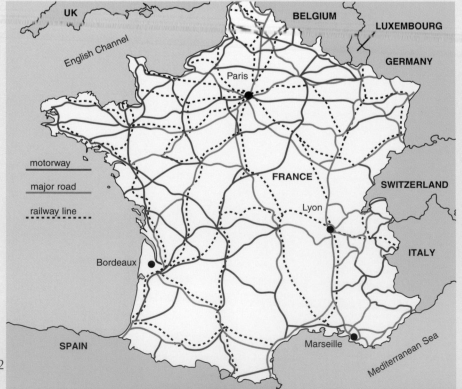

motorway
major road
railway line

UK
English Channel
BELGIUM
LUXEMBOURG
GERMANY
Paris
FRANCE
SWITZERLAND
Lyon
ITALY
Bordeaux
Marseille
Mediterranean Sea
SPAIN

The River Seine flows through the centre of Paris, France.

AROUND THE WORLD

You are going to investigate six capital cities around the world. First, look at an atlas and choose one capital city from each of the continents of Africa, North America, South America, Europe, Asia and Australasia. Using your atlas, study the location of each city. Why do you think it was chosen? Do you think it is in the best location now?

Try to find out as much as you can about each city, using guidebooks, photographs and street maps which you can find on the Internet. Which one would you most like to live in? Why?

HELPING HAND
Think about transport, communications, climate, space and overcrowding.

The National Diet (government) Building is in Tokyo, the capital city of Japan.

Growth

Most towns and cities are bigger now than at any time in the past. One reason for this is because the world's population is growing. Another reason is that people's lifestyles are changing. For example, more and more people are moving from the countryside to urban settlements to look for work, to be with other family members or to make use of better public services such as schools and hospitals.

HOW SETTLEMENTS GROW
Often settlements expand outwards. This means that the central part is usually the oldest part and the newest areas tend to be those on the outskirts. Some settlements are surrounded by plenty of available land. They can expand outwards over a huge area, creating extensive residential areas known as suburbs. Other settlements have less room to grow outwards. This may be because they are close to other settlements, or because they are surrounded by mountains or sea. When this is the case, older buildings may be knocked down and new ones built upwards, creating high-rise homes and workplaces.

The city of Mumbai in India is built on an island.

Oberoi Towers

Many poor people in Mumbai live in over-crowded shanty towns on the edges of the city.

PROBLEMS WITH GROWTH

Large settlements began as much smaller settlements. Most struggle to cope with rapid growth. Often there is not enough land for new buildings. As more people arrive, residential areas can become overcrowded. Roads become congested, and public services are overstretched. Many poor people may be forced to live in slum conditions.

Look at the photographs of Mumbai, India, and New York, USA.

You are going to compare Mumbai with New York. Look at each city on a map. They have both grown from small ports into major cities. Use the Internet and library books to find out how they are similar. How are they different? What reasons can you think of for this?

HELPING HAND
Think about natural features, industry, wealth and poverty, available land and population growth.

New York is surrounded on three sides by water.

Pollution

Pollution is anything that contaminates water, air or land. Most of the time it is some sort of waste product such as sewage, chemicals, exhaust fumes or litter. Once it enters the environment, it can be difficult to get rid of.

KEY SKILLS

Drawing a sketch map

Making a visual survey

Analysing and interpreting results

AIR POLLUTION

Air pollution is not a new problem. Ever since the industrial revolution in the nineteenth century, factories, homes and, more recently, cars have been burning fossil fuels and sending poisonous gases into the atmosphere. A century ago, London was frequently enveloped in a thick, unhealthy "smog" of fumes and smoke.

Today air pollution is a major problem for many cities. The air is filled with tiny particles that make us cough and aggravate illnesses such as asthma. Beijing in China is one of the most polluted cities, largely because of its rapid industrial growth.

HOUSEHOLD WASTE

Household waste includes paper, plastic, glass, metal and food waste. Some types of household waste can be recycled, but the rest is either burned, dumped at huge waste sites or buried underground. All these methods cause further pollution problems.

High levels of air pollution in Beijing, China, pose a serious health risk.

36

WHAT CAN WE DO?

Sometimes people can be reluctant to deal with the problem of pollution. For example, many of us like the convenience of plastic packaging and many factories burn fossil fuels because it is the cheapest way to generate energy.

Yet there are many things we can do to stop wasting resources and to reduce pollution in our towns and cities. Sometimes the simplest solutions are the most effective. Some countries, such as Ireland and South Africa, have stopped supermarkets giving away free plastic bags. Now customers have to pay for them, and this has encouraged many people to re-use their bags instead of throwing them away.

MAKING A LITTER MAP

You are going to make a "litter map" of your local high street. First, draw a sketch map of the street, showing individual shops, buildings and other structures such as bus shelters and telephone booths. Next, mark the location of any litter bins along the street. Note how full they are. Finally, highlight any litter hotspots – places where there is a high density of rubbish such as cans, wrappers, chewing gum or plastic bags. These may be outside particular shops or fast-food restaurants or bars, or at bus stops.

What does your litter map tell you? Are there enough bins? Are they in the right places? Do they need to be emptied more often, or do people need to be encouraged to use them more often? Write an action plan, suggesting three ways to reduce litter in your high street.

Waste is a source of pollution throughout the world. In the Philippines, waste pickers try to earn money by selling materials they find in rubbish thrown away by people in large cities.

HELPING HAND
Find out when any litter bins are emptied and whether the street is cleaned on any particular day of the week. Make your litter map the day before!

Poverty

One third of the world's urban population lives in poverty. Even those cities that seem wealthy and developed are home to people with no jobs, or who earn such low wages that they can barely afford to feed themselves. Why is this?

A homeless person begs on a street in Hamburg, Germany.

REASONS FOR MIGRATION

Approximately one million people around the world move from the countryside to cities each week. Most migrants live in LEDCs, but there are many in more economically developed countries (MEDCs), too. Usually they are looking for work, but often there are not enough jobs and homes for everyone.

However, not all urban poverty is due to migration and lack of jobs. Discrimination, lack of education and ill-health also play a part. So does government policy. In the 1930s, millions of people in the USA and Europe lost their jobs due to bad decisions by their governments. As a result of this, many people lost their homes and their life savings.

SLUMS AND SHANTY TOWNS

Most of the world's urban poor live in informal settlements such as slums and shanty towns. Slums are areas of run-down, overcrowded housing. Shanty towns are areas where people have built their own homes from scrap materials, often crowded together without drains, power or running water. Many of these homes are built illegally, but some of them have existed for so long that they have become permanent communities with schools and other services.

POVERTY AND DISEASE

Poverty and disease are often closely linked. Poor people in LEDCs may not have access to clean water or proper sanitation. They may not be able to afford to pay for immunisations and medicines, and those who live in overcrowded slums are most at risk from infectious diseases.

WOMEN AND POVERTY

People in cities are not the only ones at risk from the problems of poverty. Many living in rural settlements in LEDCs face similar hardships. This is particularly the case for women who live in parts of the world where they are prevented from owning land or are paid less than men for doing the same work.

There are no easy answers to the problem of poverty. Some people think that governments should act to provide jobs and build better housing. But where should the money for this come from – from charities, ordinary taxpayers or wealthy individuals?

Hold a class debate to discuss ways to deal with poverty. Choose three ways and write an action plan, setting out your proposals.

KEY SKILLS

 Looking at a global issue

 Debating solutions; listening to other points of view

People at a shanty town in Nairobi, Kenya. Over 70 per cent of the world's urban poor live in sub-Saharan Africa.

New settlements

Some settlements are deliberately planned. A site is chosen and roads, buildings and public spaces are laid out according to specific ideas about who the settlement is for and what it should be like. Town planners often aim to solve many of the problems of modern urban life.

COMPARING SETTLEMENTS

You are going to compare two settlements: Poundbury in the south of England and Almere in the Netherlands.

POUNDBURY

Poundbury is a new settlement close to the historic town of Dorchester in the south of England. It was planned as a model village community where people live and work within the same local area. The site had previously been farmland. The first stage was completed in the mid-1990s, but the settlement has been designed to grow to a maximum of 6,000 inhabitants.

Poundbury is a popular place to live – many people have moved there. However, this has caused house prices to rise, and the village planners are sometimes criticised for not allowing enough low-cost housing to be built. A relatively large number of inhabitants are retired. The gardens are small, but a substantial park is planned. Some shops, workplaces and services are situated in the village itself, with others in nearby Dorchester.

Houses in Poundbury have been built with a deliberate mixture of traditional styles and materials. Winding roads slow traffic and create a less uniform appearance.

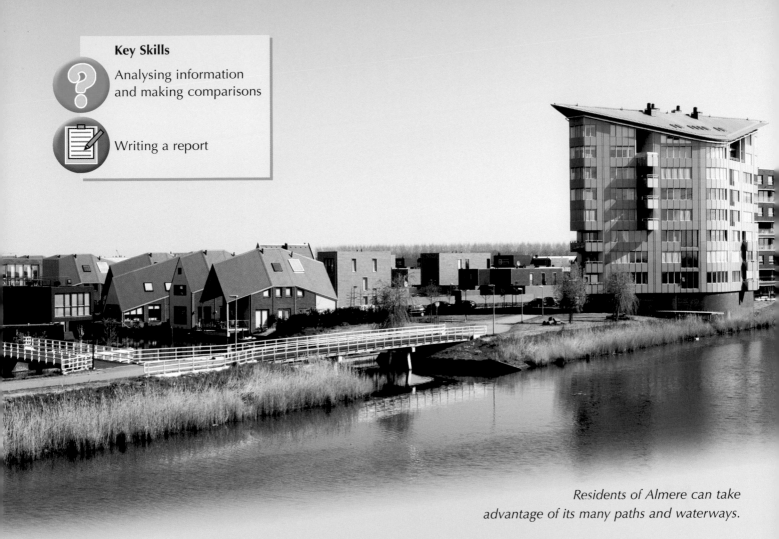

*Residents of Almere can take
advantage of its many paths and waterways.*

ALMERE

Almere was planned as a
solution to housing shortages
in nearby Amsterdam, capital
city of the Netherlands. It was
built on land reclaimed from
the mud of the Zuiderzee (an
inland sea) and the first
residents moved in during
the 1970s.

Almere was intended to be a
model suburb, with all the
advantages of space, cleaner
air and cheaper, low-rise
housing. One third of the land
was for light industry, one third
for housing and one third for
parks and open spaces. Traffic
is largely confined to outer ring
roads, and public transport
links to Amsterdam are good.

Almere expanded rapidly,
and today has a population
of about 180,000. Housing
is modern-looking and cheap
compared with other areas.
Residents have plenty of
opportunities for outdoor
activities. However, the town
has been criticised for its lack
of entertainment facilities
such as bars and nightclubs,
and some young people say
they have little to do in Almere.

Using the Internet, find out
as much as you can about
Almere and Poundbury.

What similarities can you
find between them? What are
the differences? Have the two
settlements lived up to the
ideas of the planners? Where
have the planners succeeded
and where have they failed?

Write a report explaining
which of the two settlements
you would like to live in.
You should try to find
photographs on the Internet
to support your answers.

Planning for the future

What will settlements be like in the future? We know that there will be more of them, and most of them will be larger. But will they be different in other ways?

KEY SKILLS

Researching a settlement

Writing a report

THE ENVIRONMENT

If settlements continue to expand outwards, taking up more and more of the surrounding countryside, then the open spaces between settlements will disappear altogether. This is already happening in some densely populated areas.

Many town planners now think it is better to redevelop existing urban areas, with more high-rise buildings and more compact homes with smaller gardens. A greater concentration of urban homes means that transport, energy and public services can be organised more efficiently, and there is less need to build on green-field sites.

People are also becoming more aware of environmental issues in their homes. Double-glazing, solar panels and better insulation are all ways to increase energy efficiency and cut down on pollution.

These houses in Denmark have been designed to maximise energy efficiency.

Gated communities are designed with security in mind.

VIRTUAL LIVING

The Internet and other new technologies mean that more and more people can work, shop, study, and even make friends and socialise without having to leave home. This is better for the environment, but what impact will it have on local communities?

RICH AND POOR

As we have already seen, poverty is one of the biggest challenges for urban settlements. As slums and shanty towns push up against the homes of the wealthy, the divide between rich and poor seems even more obvious. One solution to this is called "urban regeneration" where old slum buildings are pulled down and new homes and offices are built, with a view to creating socially mixed neighbourhoods. However, it can be difficult, and costly, to put this into practice.

Some people fear the crime that is associated with poverty and deprivation, and prefer to live in "gated" communities where their homes are protected by high fences and security guards. Others argue that this simply increases a sense of segregation and fear.

Try to visit your local council's planning department, or send an e-mail, to find out about future plans for the area in which you live. What are the concerns of planners? Is there anything you think they ought to be considering?

Write a brief report explaining your findings. Would you like to live there in the future?

HELPING HAND
Write down a list of four or five questions you want to ask before you visit the planning department.

Glossary

Aquifer
An underground layer of sand, gravel or rock that collects water and holds it like a giant sponge.

Atmosphere
The mixture of gases that surrounds the Earth.

Budget
The amount of money someone plans to spend on something.

Climate
The average weather conditions of a certain area.

Commute
To travel from the suburbs into the city centre to work.

Congestion charge
A fee paid by road users who travel into the city centre. Congestion charges are established so that there is less traffic in the city.

Data
Information that is analysed so that a decision can be made.

Discrimination
Treating people differently, often unfairly, because of their race, social standing, income or religion.

Drought
A long period where there is little or no rainfall.

Dysentery
An illness that causes severe diarrhoea.

Embassy
The place where a foreign government official, or ambassador, has an office.

Fossil fuels
Carbon-based fuels such as petroleum, coal and natural gas made from the remains of dead animals and plants.

Green belt
Parks, farmland and any other undeveloped land that surrounds a community.

Habitat
The environment to which a plant or an animal is best suited and where it usually grows or lives.

Hamlet
A small village.

Immunisations
Injections to prevent diseases.

Informal settlements
Self-built, illegal settlements, locally known as bustees, favelas or shanty towns.

Interdependence
When two or more things rely on each other.

Irrigate
To water the land artificially.

Isolated
To be separate and away from other people or buildings.

Leisure
How people spend their free time: sport or tourist activities, for example.

Less economically developed country (LEDC)
A country in which the majority of the population lives in poverty. These countries tend to be mainly rural, but often their cities and towns are growing fast.

Linear settlement
A type of settlement which has developed in a line, perhaps next to a river or road.

Migrant
A person who moves, or migrates, from one region or area to another.

Monsoon
A wind that blows in Asia from the southwest. Monsoons bring heavy rains in the summer.

More economically developed country (MEDC)
A country with much greater wealth per person and more developed industry than a less economically developed country.

Natural resource
A material or substance such as timber, fresh water, or a mineral deposit, that occurs naturally and has an economic value.

Nucleated settlement
A type of settlement that has grown around a central point, such as a town square or church.

Origin
Where something began.

Recycle
To collect useful materials, such as glass and paper, and reprocess them into something else so that they can be used again.

Regeneration
When something is changed for the better.

Reservoir
A pond or lake used to store water.

Sanitation
The drainage and disposal of sewage.

Terraced houses
Houses with shared walls, built in rows.

Town planners
The people who plan the layout and development of new settlements.

Weblinks

www.nationalgeographic.com/3cities
Look at cities during three different millennia, including Alexandria in Egypt, Cordoba in Spain and New York, USA.

www.worldcityphotos.org
A large collection of photographs of cities from around the world, listed by country.

www.ngfl-cymru.org.uk/vtc-home/vtc-ks3-home
Go to "Geography", then "Settlement", then "Settlement patterns in Wales". Click on "Aerial photographs" for excellent images of different types of settlement.

www.globalvillage2006.org
This website gives you lots of ideas about how you can make a difference to problems such as poverty and disease.

www.theory.tifr.res.in/bombay/
A comprehensive site with information on all aspects of Mumbai, including geography, population and growth.

www.cclondon.com
Official multi-lingual site with information on congestion charging and other transport issues in London, as well as maps and photographs.

http://geography.about.com/library/maps/blindex.htm
Go to "World Atlas & Maps" for a wide variety of maps for every country in the world.

www.planning.org/KidsAndCommunity/index.htm
A fun, interactive site for children to explore the ways in which our towns and cities are planned.

Note to parents and teachers:

Every effort has been made by the Publishers to ensure that these websites are suitable for children, that they are of the highest educational value, and that they contain no inappropriate or offensive material. However, because of the nature of the Internet, it is impossible to guarantee that the contents of these sites will not be altered. We strongly advise that Internet access is supervised by a responsible adult.

Index

THE PRIVATE EYE ANNUAL 2003

EDITED BY IAN HISLOP

ALTHOUGH TARZAN WAS RAISED IN THE JUNGLE BY APES, HE WAS STILL BRITISH

Published in Great Britain by
Private Eye Productions Ltd
6 Carlisle Street, London W1D 5BN

© 2003 Pressdram Ltd
ISBN 1 901784 31 2
Designed by Bridget Tisdall
Printed in England by
Goodman Baylis Ltd, Worcester

2 4 6 8 10 9 7 5 3 1

THE PRIVATE EYE ANNUAL 2003

EDITED BY IAN HISLOP

*"Oh, look! My fag packet is beating your lager can and
Piglet's empty gluetube"*

A NATIONWIDE poll of our readers reveals for the first time the ten greatest Britons who ever lived. Now the case for each of them is argued by one of the Eye's top columnists.

PRIVATE EYE'S TOP TEN BRITONS

PRINCESS DIANA

by Polly Filler

1 SAINT DIANA was the greatest feminist icon of all time. She not only changed Britain for ever. She had the most wonderful dress sense and looked good in photographs – like me.

ROBERT MAXWELL

by Lord Gnome

2 BOB MAXWELL was a towering genius who revolutionised the British press. He alone came up with the ground-breaking financial strategy of stealing money from the newspaper pension fund. If he had a weakness, it was his failure to learn to swim.

KARL MARX

by Dave Spart

3 ONLY a racist and xenophobe would disqualify Marx on the Little Englander grounds that he was German... er... he was the greatest philosopher who ever lived and if only his ideas had been put into practice the world would... er...

DAVID BECKHAM

by Glenda Slagg

4 MMMMM, don't-chajustlovehim? With his little-boy smile and beefcake body, he's the Number One Hunk of all time. Hats (and everything else!) off to the man who's got us all United (geddit?!?!)

JOHN LENNON

by E.J. Thribb*

5 LENNON was the greatest poet who ever lived. When he died, I wrote the following tribute, which says it all:

So. Farewell then John Lennon.

Imagine there's no Heaven.

That was your Catchphrase.

And now you don't Have to imagine it Any more.

* E.J. Thribb is sponsored by Lemsip

IAIN DUNCAN SMITH

by Peter O'Bore

6 IAIN is the quiet man of British politics. His towering strengths have not yet shown themselves. But when they do, he will prove himself an even greater Briton than Churchill, Gladstone, Disraeli and Queen Elizabeth the First.

DAME BARBARA CARTLAND

by Sylvie Krin

7 AS THE first rays of soft autumn sunshine steal over my word processor, my thoughts inevitably turn to the greatest writer this sceptred isle has ever produced. I refer of course to that supreme chronicler of the human heart *(That's enough. Ed.)*

THE AYATOLLAH KHOMEINI

by The Rev. J.C. Flannel

8 AT A TIME when we are all becoming more aware of each other's faiths in the multi-cultural society that is Britain today, surely the greatest Briton of all must be the late Ayatollah Khomeini. His message of peace and universal brotherhood still speaks to us today, whatever our colour, creed or sexual orientation.

LORD JENKINS

by Roy Jenkins

9 FAR BE IT from me to blow my own twumpet, an always unattwactive twait in any chwonicler of the passing pawade of our pwoud histowy. Yet when I consider my own mewits, albeit weluctantly, I am forced to conclude that, as a statesman, wwiter, histowian and, may I say, connoisseur of clawet, my claims to be considered as the gweatest Bwiton of all are by no means inconsidewable.

PHIL MITCHELL

by Phil Space

10 NO LIST of the greatest Britons in history would be complete without the bulldog presence of the greatest Briton who ever lived – Phil Mitchell from *EastEnders*. It was his unflinching courage in the dark days of 1940 which (cont'd p. 94)

THAT GREAT BRITONS LIST IN FULL

(continued from page 1)

ONE YEAR ON

Private Eye's special 911-page supplement to commemorate the anniversary of the earthquake that shook the world

IT IS exactly one year ago that the world changed for ever when, totally out of the blue, Iain Duncan Smith became leader of the Conservative Party.

Private Eye asked a group of top opinion-formers to look back over the momentous events which followed the cataclysm that became known to the world simply as "13/11".

Lord Rees-Mogg
(antiquarian bookseller in West Country):

IT WAS totally unexpected. Even I didn't predict it, with my long experience of getting everything wrong. Even in Somerset, people didn't quite know how to react. Some people went to church to pray. Others sat in their studies writing columns for the Times.

Richard Harries, Bishop of Oxford
(author and broadcaster):

IT WAS a terrible shock. Many people asked me in the days that followed, "If there is a God, Bishop, why does he allow this sort of thing to happen?" It's never easy for a Christian to answer that one. But I think what we can say, very definitely, is that God moves in a mysterious way and it is not always open to us to know why certain things happen in the way they do."

Christine Hamilton
(Television personality):

IT WAS just awful. This great edifice, which we'd all grown up with as part of the scenery, suddenly it was gone. Just a hole where it used to be. Even now I can't take it in. These people just wiped out the whole Tory Party, just like that. When I see the film of it on television, it makes me shudder. I still can't believe that it happened.

Christopher "The Hitch" Hitchens
(Professor of Martin Amis Studies at the University of Burger King):

WHEN they flagged up on the scoreboard that the most impossible thing in the world had suddenly become not just possible but horrifyingly only too actual, the emotions go into overdrive, taking in the whole gamut of human emotion from A to B. I'm sorry, what am I writing about again?

Boris Johnson
(editor of the Beano and Tory MP for Henley-on-Toast):

BLIMEY! Cripes! Duncan Smith! I mean, who'd have thought it! Still, it makes you think! If they could go for an obvious no-hoper like Duncan whatever-his-name, then why not me? Tally ho! "Beano Boris" for PM!

Iain Duncan Smith *(party leader):*
NO COMMENT.

TUBE DRIVERS BRING CHAOS TO LONDON

by Our Transport Staff **Lester Square**

ANGRY commuters trying to get to work this morning were confronted by scenes of massive disruption as tube drivers worked normally.

Trains were mostly late or cancelled and the few that ran on time were hopelessly overcrowded.

One commuter said, "It's a disgrace. They have a responsibility to the public and they should have stayed on strike, allowing travellers to get to work on time by foot."

Said a furious nurse, "I was late for my ward duties this morning simply because these greedy tube drivers went to work for a day."

Northern Lie-in

However, the Mayor of London, Mr Kensington Livingwell, told reporters, "I think public transport is working very well, but I am in Brighton."

Union leader Mr Bob Spart remained defiant and threatened commuters with worse to come. "My members will probably go to work one day next week," he said, "and there could be further days of work right up to Christmas."

BRITAIN ROCKED BY HUGE HEADLINE

PEOPLE in the UK were last night still in shock after being hit by a series of huge newspaper headlines carrying news of a relatively small, localised earth tremor.

Said one onlooker, "I picked up the newspaper, and there was this huge, earth-shattering headline which left me literally quaking in my boots – it was just like that film when all those houses disappear and thousands of people, get killed, except it wasn't at all really." *(A.P.)*

"Sorry to trouble you but could you recharge my mobile?"

SADDAM 'ONLY HOURS AWAY' FROM NUKING WORLD

by Our Terror Staff **Melanie Flips**

A TERRIFYING report, published today by the prestigious Institute You've Never Heard Of Before, reveals that Saddam Hussein could be on the verge of achieving full nuclear capability at any time in the next few weeks.

"All he has to do," says the report, "is to acquire the nuclear materials, assemble an expert team capable of putting all the pieces together, and he could then have a fully operational nuclear device within a matter of only ten years or so."

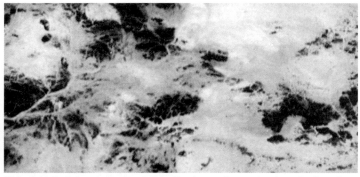

This aerial picture clearly shows the type of remote desert site where Saddam could be planning to install the launching pads from which nuclear missiles aimed at Britain could be fired. (Reuters)

BUSH DOSSIER SHOCK

THE Bush Administration has made public a dossier that reveals that Saddam Hussein has over the last few years amassed a huge stockpile of both biological and non-biological washing powder.

"We believe these stockpiles could be used either to launch a massive first strike against targets throughout the West, or to do his cotton shirts," said a clearly shaken U.S. President...
(cont. p. 94)

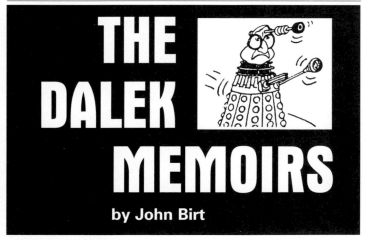

THE DALEK MEMOIRS

by John Birt

■ EXCLUSIVE to Private Eye – Britain's former chief Dalek looks back on his years as Director General of the Dalek Corporation.

Chapter One

My plan was to exterminate the BBC in three stages: Exterminate. Exterminate. Exterminate.

TOMORROW: How I introduced 24-hour rolling Daleks and purchased an Armani Dalek suit and put it on expenses.

© Birtdrivel 2002.

NURSERY TIMES

Friday September 20 2002

DID COW *REALLY* JUMP OVER MOON?

by Our Astronomy Staff **Phil Space**

THE WORLD of Nursery Rhymes was rocked last night when it was claimed that the famous cow moon jump never took place.

Disbelievers are now claiming that the whole thing was a hoax designed to get one up on the Jumblies and their record-breaking, round-the-world sieve voyage.

Said one sceptic, "The pictures of the cow sailing over the moon are obviously faked. The way the light from the moon is shining on the cow *proves* that no jump ever took place."

The furious jump veteran, Mr Buzz Moo, 79, hit out at his critics and felled them with his hoof.

Lunacy

"This makes me mad," he said. "My mission to the moon was witnessed by a laughing little dog and a fiddle-playing cat. What more proof do you need?"

Neither dog nor cat, however, were yesterday available for comment.

LATE NEWS

☐ Dish and spoon to split

☐ Dish insists that his sperm is destroyed. Full story "Me and My Spoon" **94**

"Of course, you must bear in mind we've not got a 100 percent success in reuniting couples"

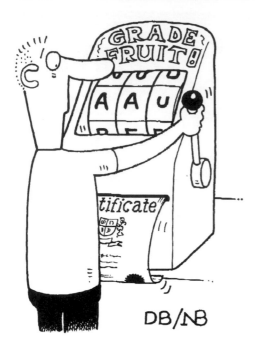

DB/NB

There are lies, exam lies and statistics

School news

St Cakes

Pederast Term begins today. There are three suspects in the school. Mr Peter File is the new head of computer studies. Gropings will be on December 3rd. *(That's enough St Cocks. Ed.)*

That Slade Honorary Degree Citation in Full

SALUTAMUS SLADUM, GROUPUM POPULARUM CANTORUM DE WOLVERHAMPTIONE CONURBATIONE IN 'TERRA NIGRA' APPELATUS, TERRIBILIS GLAMI ROCKERI IN DECADO MCMLXX-MCMLXXX, FAMOSISSIMUS PER SINGULUS CELEBRATENS FESTIVALIS DIES NATALIS JESUM CHRISTUM: "HIC EST JOVIALIS XMASENSIS ET OMNES GAUDENT". DISCUS COMPULSORIUS PER MULTOS ANNOS IN PRECINCTIS MERCUNTALIBUS, EG, BRENTUS CROSSUS, PARTICULARE IN OMNES TESCONES, WOOLIES, MARCUS SPARKUSQUE. LUDET CONSTANTER IN RADIO DUO WOGANENSIS. SALUTAMUS NODDIUS HOLDERUS (PRIMUS CANTORUS), DAVUS HILLUS (PRIMUS GUITARUS), JIMMUS LEA (SECUNDUS GUITARUS), DONNUS POWELLIUS (PERCUSSIONIS).

© The University of Wolverhampton
(formerly Wrekin and Telford New Town Polytechnic).

BUSH'S NEW INITIATIVE

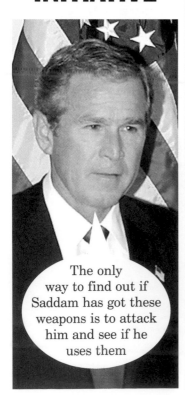

The only way to find out if Saddam has got these weapons is to attack him and see if he uses them

DOES SADDAM POSSESS A MOUSTACHE?

by Our Defence Staff
Brig. John Trumper-Smythe

THE DOSSIER released last week by Tony Blair contains conclusive evidence that Saddam Hussein has the capacity to grow a moustache within 48 hours.

In fact he may already have one.

Intelligence reports from deep inside Iraq suggest that the Iraqi Moustache Project (codenamed SADMOUST) is already highly advanced.

Details of the project could not be included in the dossier in case they compromised valuable intelligence sources (poss. G. Bush).

Cat and Moustache

Saddam has a long history of playing "cat and mouse" games with UN Moustache Inspectors. Sometimes they are allowed into the Presidential Palace – at other times they are told that it is closed "for repairs".

Said one former inspector: "Saddam cannot be trusted. He could easily have a moustache by now. But we would not necessarily know."

● That moustache dossier in full 2-94

PRINCE CHARLES' HISTORY LESSON

It should be about Kings and Queens and Princes, who all too easily get forgotten...

HIGHLIGHTS FROM THE BLAIR DOSSIER

No. 94 Range of Saddam's Ballistic Missiles

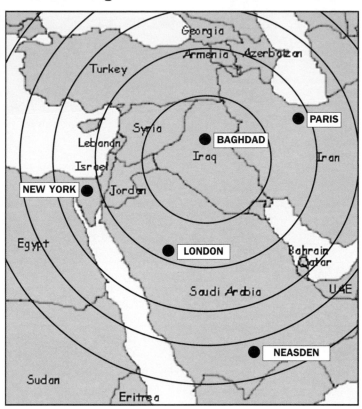

No. 95 The Al Fayed Shufti-Bastad Liquid Nuclear Anthrax Facility in Tariqali

Ⓐ **Toilet Block** Ⓑ **Cricket Pavilion** Ⓒ **Pirate Treasure**

AN APOLOGY
Gordon Brown

IN COMMON with all other newspapers we may have given the impression that Mr Gordon Brown was the most capable Chancellor of the Exchequer in history, who had single-handedly put an end to the boom-and-bust disasters of former years and built up such a gigantic financial surplus that he could afford to hand out billions of pounds to schools and hospitals and still have plenty left over. Headlines such as 'Super-Gordon Does It Again', 'Cash Gordon Saves The World" and 'Brown Puts UK In The Black', may have led readers to believe that we in some way entertained the notion that Mr Brown was a financial genius of the highest order.

We now realise that Mr Brown is in fact little more than a financial nincompoop who has somehow managed to get his sums wrong to the tune of a staggering £7 billion and that his public spending plans are therefore headed for total disaster. We are happy to put the record straight and to apologise unreservedly to Mr Brown for having suggested that he had the slightest idea what he was up to.

NOW IT'S A NASTY COUGH!

by Our Political Staff **Meg O'Zone**

THE LEADER of the Conservative Party, Mr Iain Duncan Cough, has at last broken his long silence by launching an astonishing personal attack on the prime minister, Mr Tony Blair.

In one of the most outspoken broadsides in parliamentary history, Mr Cough accused Mr Blair of being "absolutely right" in his support for President Bush's plans to attack Saddam Hussein.

Cough lashed out, "Mr Blair has shown great personal courage in backing this war, but he has not gone nearly far enough.

RespiraTory Complaint

"My opinion, for what it's worth, is that we should do everything President Bush and Mr Blair suggest, but also quite a lot more."

When he was pressed by reporters to be more specific he quickly silenced them by reverting to his earlier policy of saying nothing at all.

Mr Duncan Cough is hopeless *(Surely '47'? Ed.).*

THE DAILY TELEGRAPH Friday, October 18, 2002

Charles Moore Beatification
Controversy Grows

BY OUR RELIGIOUS CORRESPONDENT CHRISTOPHER BEARDIE

The leader of the sinister Opus Dailytelegraph movement has been made a saint in a surprise move that has shocked many Catholics.

"Normally, a saint has to be associated with a miracle," said one of the faithful, "but Moore's so-called miracle of putting on five thousand readers is a sham.

"We all know that he just handed out free newspapers on the Inter-City trains."

Fact

● Opus Dailytelegraph is run by a fanatical group of right-wing Conservatives, many of whom went to school together at Eton.

● Opus Dailytelegraph is devoted to the worship of Liz Hurley, whom its members believe to have miraculous powers to restore the newspaper's circulation.

● The Opus Dailytelegraph has its tentacles right through the British Establishment. Among its devotees are Sir Herbert Gussett, Sir Peregrine Worsthorne, Sir Max Hastings and the Venerable Deede, the 109-year-old guru whose longevity is one of the mysteries at the heart of the Opus Dailytelegraph.

'Save The Telegraph'
YOUR 94-PAGE PULL-OUT SUPPLEMENT

Millions March Through London
by Our Entire Staff

Well over half the population of Britain turned out yesterday to proclaim their support for the Daily Telegraph.

Under the banner 'Life and Liz Hurley', they came from all four corners of Britain and marched with heads held high through the heart of London.

Wife and Liberty's Sale

When the numbers reached 50 million, a great cheer went up which could be heard as far away as Land's End.

All ages were on the march – teenagers in their blue jeans mingled with old-age pensioners in their barbours and woolly socks, wealthy landowners with people who only buy it for the crossword.

But all of them were united in their passionate defence of one of England's oldest freedoms – "The right to read the Daily Telegraph".

"He's re-booting his computer"

The Grauniad

The Left To March

WHEN thousands of people march through the streets of London to protest about Government policy, Mr Blair must sit up and take notice, unless of course they are wearing wellingtons, in which case they are probably "in-bred lunatics and Hooray Henrys who should be ignored or possibly locked up". (©Rod Liddle, *Grauniad* 2002.)

No, this latest march with its solid citizens carrying sensible banners, such as "Bush Is Hitler" and "Support Saddam Now", represents a political sea-change of *(p. 94)*

A Man of Letters

by Dame Sylvie Krin

Best-selling author of "La Dame Aux Camillas", "Heir of Sorrows" and "Tampax Britannica"

THE STORY SO FAR: Camilla is still seething over Charles's refusal to allow her to join the Countryside March.

Now read on..

CHARLES SAT at his Louis Theroux escritoire in the study at Highgrove, musing on what would be the subject of his next letter to the Lord Chancellor, Lord Lairgover.

His gaze wandered through the open window to the long drive and the avenue of ancient haw trees, their leaves already tinged with the golden hues of autumn.

Down the lane hummed the electric milk-float from the organic dairy with old Dimbleby at the wheel.

That was it! That was what had been annoying him. At last the Muse had descended like a ripened conker onto the verdant lawn.

Seizing his Dennis Waterman fountain pen, a gift from his art tutor, the late Sir Hugh Casson, he began to scribble furiously in his spidery hand...

Dear Lord Chancellor,
You will remember that when we met yesterday you very kindly asked me to let you know of any further concerns on my part about, you know, the whole collapse of this Britain thingy.

Well, it suddenly struck me that one of our biggest problems is those new-fangled cardboard milk cartons. They're absolutely impossible to open without spilling milk all over your waistcoat! It really is appalling.

Why can't they have glass bottles, like in the old days?
Yours sincerely,
Charles

With a sigh of contentment, Charles sat back and re-read his latest missive.

Yes, this would get Blair's government back on the right track. Everything in the garden would be lovely.

"EVERYTHING in the garden is lovely." Charles had found Camilla on the Laurens van der Post memorial bench in the Islamic parterre. She sat alone, puffing at her Gilbert and George Navy-Cut cigarette.

"Come on, old girl, you're not still angry with me about the march thingy, are you?"

Camilla took a deep drag of the cigarette and blew the acrid smoke in Charles's face.

"No, I'm not angry with you, Charles. I'm just not speaking to you."

Charles coughed, waving the smoke from his face. "Look, I thought I explained all this – in my position, if you want to change things, you can't be seen marching up and down the street with banners."

Her frosty expression seemed to be melting as she listened to his words of wisdom. Encouraged, he pressed on.

"You see, in this country, everything is done quietly, behind the scenes. A word in someone's ear from a chap to another chap. Or a letter, marked Private & Confidential, to the Lord Chancellor."

Now Camilla seemed to be fully engaged. Her eyes lit up.

"This is most interesting, Chazza." She stubbed out her cigarette with the heel of her shiny Lycett-Green riding boot. "And is that one of those letters you've got there?"

"Yes," Charles replied.

"Well, I'll post it for you, darling. On my walk into Cirencester. It's such a nice day and I need to stretch my legs."

Charles was delighted by this sudden change of mood. "Thanks a lot."

"THANKS a lot!" Charles took the ironed copy of the Sunday Telegraph from the manicured hands of Sir Alan Fitztightly and joined Camilla at the breakfast table.

"What's up, darling?" Camilla smiled solicitously. "You look as if someone's poisoned your organic free-range cornflakes."

Charles slumped into his chair limply, pointing at the hurtful headline that had taken the wind from his royal sails.

HAS HE GONE LETTER MAD?

"Look at this, Cazza. It's all here. My private letter. Printed in full. And a picture of me looking completely bonkers."

Camilla said nothing, pouring herself another cup of Rhodesian Roast black coffee.

"Who could have leaked this? Somebody is trying to make me look a complete fool."

"It's obviously someone at their end, isn't it?" she soothed, patting his hand. "Nobody here would do such a thing."

She got up and walked to the window.

Yes, thought Charles. She was probably right. Someone at their end. Someone in the Government. But then he caught sight of Camilla's reflection in the glass. And wasn't that a smile playing about her cherry-red lips?

Suddenly, the bright morning sun was eclipsed by a dark cloud and the room went very cold.

(To be continued)

The Secret DIARY OF JOHN MAJOR aged 59½

Saturday morning

I am not inconsiderably incandescent with fury. I read in the Times that Mrs Currie had a passionate 4-year affair with me when I was Chief Whip. How dare she go round telling newspapers a load of truth, after we had agreed that I had drawn a line under this unfortunate event? There is only one word to describe Mrs Currie and that is BASTARD.

In fact, I have got out my old Bastard Book (which I thought I would never have to use again) and I have written her name in enormous capital letters with my special NatWest red biro.

In my judgement, her behaviour has been in no small measure disgraceful and I was quite right not to mention her in my memoirs, not even in the index. This demonstrated convincingly that she was a bastard, which of course she is.

This newspaper revelation has had a very unfortunate effect on my wife Norman. I found her in tears at the breakfast table, the Times spread out over the bowl of Golden Grahams.

"Don't cry, Norman," I said. "It was all a long time ago and I told you I had drawn a line under Mrs Currie."

"I am not crying," Norman said, wiping the tears from her eyes with her free NatWest napkin. "It is just the funniest thing I have read for years."

Clearly shock and sadness over Mrs Currie's disloyalty have turned her mind.

"It says here you were a sexual athlete, John," she said, holding her sides and starting to cry again.

Saturday afternoon

I was in no small measure even more not inconsiderably incandescent to be visited by my brother Terry who came round with a curry and a silly smile on his face.

"I thought you might enjoy this, John," he said. "It is hot and spicy!"

"I have no idea what you are talking about," I replied, as I shut the door in his face.

"Ha ha ha, John," he continued in a considerably unamusing way, shouting through the letter-box. "Remember Mrs Kierens? And how you used to nip round there for tea and crumpets after school? You always were one for the ladies. It's true what they say. It's the boring quiet ones with the glasses who are at it like rabbits all the time."

So saying, he drove off in his white van, leaving an obscene gnome on the lawn holding something that was clearly not a fishing rod.

I have immediately inserted Terry's name in my book under BB, standing for Bastard Brothers.

Sunday

The phone has not inconsiderably stopped ringing. Oh yes.

Mr Yeo was the first, followed by Mr Norris, Mr Hartley Booth, Mr Spring, Mr Hughes, Mr Richards, Mr Merchant, Mr Ashby and various other Conservative MPs who I sadly had to let go, due to their moral failings.

All of them were in tears, just like Norman. "Ha ha ha," said Mr Yeo. "We are so sorry that it had to come out now rather than at the time when you would have lost your job and we would have had Michael Heseltine instead of you, which would have been..."

"I am sorry – I am drawing a line under this conversation," I said, replacing the receiver.

Monday morning

There are no words to describe the level of my incandescence. Just when I was opening my ringbinder from Rymans to familiarise myself with my speech to the Utah Chamber of Commerce on the theme of "Probity in Public Office", the doorbell rang and who should be there but my old cook from Number 10.

"I am the one who you told to make lots of money by suing the newspapers," said Mrs Latimer. "So I have made you something very appropriate for your supper."

"It is most kind," I said.

"No, it isn't," she said. "It's Spotted Dick." Then she broke down in tears, falling about and gasping for breath, saying "Ha ha ha ha".

Monday afternoon

The last person I expected to call me has just done so.

"Guess what colour knickers I am wearing?" I knew at once it was Mrs Currie. "Grey," I said, it being the only colour I could think of.

"Wrong," she said. "I am not wearing any knickers at all!"

"I have no longer any interest in such matters," I told her in my stern, statesmanlike voice which I used at Maastricht. "I have drawn a line under your underwear many years ago."

"I am so sorry, John," she said. "I did not do it for the money – not entirely, anyway. And it makes you look a more rounded, complex and attractive figure in the eyes of history."

"I am deeply ashamed of this event and I have drawn a line under the line I drew before," I told her.

"But why didn't you ever mention me in your book?" she asked.

"I **have** put you in my book," I said. "You are in my Bastard Book. Oh yes. In capital letters with a whole page to yourself."

"I quit my job at the carwash, I left my momma a goodbye note. By sundown I'd left Kingston with my guitar under my coat. I hitch-hiked all the way down to Memphis, got a room at the YMCA. For the next three weeks I went haunting them nightclubs, looking for a place to play. Well, I thought my picking would set 'em on fire but nobody wanted to hire a guitar man. So that's when I got a job here, stacking shelves"

BRITAIN'S TOP SEXUAL ATHLETE

Oh yes!
Oh yes!
Oh yes!

Film of the Week
C4, 7pm

"Un Homme et Deux Femmes"

CLASSIC French film grise about a ménage à trois that turns sour. Starring Jean Majeur, Norma Majeur and femme fatale Salmonella Curé. Contains the classic scene where Jean carefully removes his trousers and puts them in the trouser press (Le Courbet) before making passionate love to Salmonella, using a strawberry and a copy of the Maastricht Treaty.

Eye rating: ☺☺☺☺☺

"To evict Scott call 0901 443321, to evict Oates call 0901 443322, to evict Bowers call 0901 443323, to evict Evans call 0901 443324..."

Conference Report

'WE ARE NOT THE NAZI PARTY'
Theresa May's Shock Claim

by Our Political Staff **Peter O'Bore**

DRESSED only in leopard-skin accessories, the Tory chairwoman astonished delegates to the Tory Party Conference (Sir Sidney and Lady Doris Bonkers) by announcing that the Conservative Party was no longer the "Nazi Party" and that it had been a mistake to allow people to think that the party was bent on world-domination and racial purity.

The Single European Mother

"That may have been how things were during the 12-year tyranny of Herr Thatchler, the Iron Führer," said Mother Theresa, "But all that has now changed. We are caring, compassionate and very keen on single mothers, whatever they are."

MEL SELLS GOD SQUAD PIC FLICK

Los Angeles, Tuesday

MEL GIBSON is to produce a new film of the life of Christ called "Passionheart", which tells the story of plucky Jesus H. Christ (Mel Gibson), the Australian-American freedom fighter who takes on the might of the British Empire and is brutally murdered at the hands of snobby colonial governor Sir Pontius Pilate (Charles Dance).

Christ assembles a hand-picked team of rebels, including Matthew (Matt Damon), Mark (Ben Affleck), wise-cracking Luke (Luke Perry) and evangelist John (Denzel Washington), but is betrayed by the weasly English psychopath Judas (Jude Law).

Can the love of Mary Magdalen (Gwyneth Paltrow) save Christ from the hands of the brutal British soldiers, commanded by Centurion Maximumus Anglicus Bastardus (Tom Wilkinson)?

In an explosive finale, Christ is martyred but the spirit of christianity triumphs and the evil British empire collapses for ever.

MELLOR BACKS MAJOR

Edwina is a cheap trollop

More your type really

"Whoops, I'll just turn the pressure down a tad"

13

Daily Mail

Following A Great Tradition

TODAY the Daily Mail is proud to publish the prison diaries of one of Britain's greatest novelists.

There is a long and glorious tradition of writers who have produced some of their finest and most profound work in the confinement of the prison cell.

One thinks of Boethius, Cervantes, Bunyan, Dostoievsky, Solzhenitsyn and Oscar Wilde.

Obviously, one doesn't think of Jeffrey Archer – but we have to think of some historical justification for printing this tedious and self-serving drivel.

What You Couldn't Be Bothered To Read

Jeffrey Archole reveals the living hell that is Britain's prison system.

THE BELMARSH GULAG

Day One

PRISON is a more shocking place than I had ever dreamed of. For a start, it is full of criminals, although most of them are totally innocent, like me.

In prison you are kept locked up in a "cell". This is a tiny room with a locked door and bars over the windows.

The bed you sleep on is very hard, and the food is, quite honestly, disgusting.

The worst thing about being in gaol is that you are not allowed out, even at the weekends. **Does the Home Secretary know this?**

When I get out, I have promised my fellow prisoners that I will make a speech in the House of Lords to get this evil prison system abolished.

The prisoners are guarded night and day by uniformed men whose only job is to watch you all the time, even when you are eating or writing your memoirs. It is an outrage. **Are you listening, Mr Blunkett?**

One of my fellow prisoners (whom I shall call "Made Up") told me his shocking and heart-rending story.

"Jeff," he said. "I have read all your books, and I think you are a genius.

"But, more than that, I believe that you are totally innocent and the judge who sent you down should be strung up. I can kill him for you when I get out, because that's the only language these judges understand."

© Dacretrash Productions

■ *TOMORROW: An exclusive interview with Lady Archole, who reveals that her husband is on hunger strike and has only hours to live.*

Important Statement

The Daily Mail wishes to make clear that we have not paid any money to Lord Archole for the above extracts from his prison diaries. Instead we have offered him hard drugs and the services of prostitutes to the value of £200 million.

'WHY I AM NOT LIKE ARCHER'

Mr Toad Hits Out

by Our Riverbank Correspondent Adrian Mole

A FURIOUS Mr Toad last night angrily denied that he was in any way similar to the disgraced Tory peer Jeffrey Archer.

Said Mr Toad, speaking to journalists from Toad Hall, "There is no comparison between the irrepressible, charming myself and the despicable liar Lord Archer."

Mr Toad even produced a list detailing the complete lack of similarity between their two characters.

THAT LIST IN FULL

1. Mr Toad expressed remorse for his crime.

2. Mr Toad did not spend the whole of *Wind in the Willows* attacking the judge for being biased.

3. Mr Toad does not have a wife who goes on television pretending he has been unfairly treated and that he should not have been sent to jail.

4. Mr Toad was not involved in any dodgy share dealings, shoplifting of suits, fiddling of expenses, meeting with prostitutes, issuing bogus writs against newspapers, lying, cheating, etc, etc.

5. Mr Toad is a lovable character whom people like.

6. Mr Toad is an amphibian, whereas Lord Archer is a reptile.

When asked what he thought of Lord Archer's prison diary, a disgusted Mr Toad commented drily, "It's a load of poop poop."

ST CAKES EXAM FURY

by Our Educational Staff **Barbara Alevel**

THE Headmaster of Britain's prestigious West Midlands independent boarding school St Cakes hit out today at Britain's examiners.

Said R.J. Kipling *(Motto: Exceedingly Good St Cakes)*, "This year's A-Levels are a complete scandal. The Government has clearly interfered to falsify the grades."

A-Level Playing Field

Kipling cited the case of one sixth-former, Kenya-born J.P. Kilimanjaro-Barkworth, who had been awarded an A grade in Psychology by the examiners, when he should clearly have been given a U.

"This boy," said the Head–master, "is as thick as two short planks. Yet the examiners have given him an A grade.

"Now he has lost the chance to go into the City and will be forced to go to University instead. It is little short of a tragedy for him and for the school.

"We at St Cakes are known for the high standard of our fees. This sort of thing is not going to help."

LATE NEWS

A-Level to be replaced by new U-Level **94**

Page 94 to be regraded down to page 49 . . . . **49**

"If you keep studying for your A levels you'll never get to university"

Russell.

ESTELLE MORRIS SHOCK

You are a complete failure

I demand a regrade

ART WORLD IN 'BULLSHIT' STORM

by Our Art Staff **Brian Arsewoman**

A PROMINENT modern artist was at the centre of a furious row last night after denouncing New Labour as "conceptual bullshit".

The artist pinned a note to the door of 10 Downing Street which read, "Your stuff is all just empty, meaningless concepts which are poorly executed with unimpressive results. A child of four could do better. If this is all Britain can produce then we are all in deep elephant dung."

The Tony Prize

A spokesman for Ten Modern (formerly "Number Ten Downing Street") said: "New Labour's work is designed to challenge people's assumptions that the government is capable of doing anything."

Old People's Home

"We're going to have to ask you to leave, Mr Lee – we've just found out you're only 38"

That Jeffrey Archer Lincoln Restaurant Menu in full

Porridge

– ❋ –

Jailbait

– ❋ –

Mr Toad In A Hole

– ❋ –

Gillian Shephard's Pie

– ❋ –

Banged-Up and Mash

– ❋ –

Just Desserts
Spotted Back

– ❋ –

To Drink
Mary Archer Whine

Police Cars at 1.30

WAS THIS THE WORLD'S FIRST TORY?

by Our Archaeological Staff **Miss I.N.G. Link**

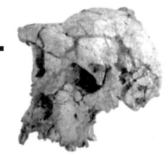

THE archaeological world was thrown into turmoil yesterday by the discovery in Bournemouth of the perfectly preserved skull of what some experts believe to be the world's oldest Conservative.

The skull, belonging to a creature dubbed by scientists as *Homophobicus normotebbitus*, has sparked fierce debate as rival experts contest whether it is genuinely human or not.

Chingford Man

Said Professor Oliver Leftwing, "This creature had a very small brain and a limited series of reflexes. It's no wonder he became extinct."

But other archaeologists, led by Professor C.J.P. Kilimanjaro-Barkworth, maintain that the so-called Chingford Man was capable of getting on his bicycle and looking for work.

Norman Tebbit is 7 million years old.

On Other Pages

Your brains tonight **20**

15

EXCLUSIVE TO PRIVATE EYE

■ *In a sensational exclusive interview with Private Eye, royal butler PAUL BURRELL reveals to the world for the first time the full details of his top-secret three-hour in-depth heart-to-heart interview with Her Majesty the Queen.*

You'll never pin this one on me, Ma'am

I SHALL never forget the day when Her Majesty the Queen rang up to ask me round to the Palace to, as she put it, "have a little chat".

When I was shown in to her drawing room at the Palace, there were just the two of us.

Me and the Queen of England. Asking for my advice.

I have often heard it said that the Queen is cold and aloof.

This is completely untrue, as she asked me to wait half-an-hour for her to finish her luncheon.

Made It Up

"Paul," she said, calling me by my christian name and offering me a place to stand on the carpet, "you are the most loyal of all the royal servants, and I really appreciate all that you have done for Diana and the whole of our family."

From these words, it should be clear that there was no feud between the two women, as so many people have alleged.

I know this because I served both of them, although I am too loyal even to comment on this publicly in a newspaper.

The Queen then asked me whether I was still looking after any of the late Princess's personal effects.

"Indeed, Ma'am, I am," I told her, "and I regard it as a sacred trust to guard her property in perpetuity for the sake of posterity."

There was no doubting the look of gratitude which came over Her Majesty's face, as she realised that I was truly the rock on which the whole ship of Britain's monarchy would founder. *(Surely "could safely rest"? Ed.)*

Before our historic interview was terminated, Her Majesty placed a finger to her lips and gave me an astonishing warning.

"Paul," she said, "it is very dark outside this room. I am very worried that you might fall downstairs and be killed, before you can sell your story to Private Eye."

© *Roll Out The Burrell Productions.*

Why I Chose Private Eye To Tell My Story

As told by Paul Burrell to Phil Space

I HAVE had many offers for my story from the world's media.

But I had no hesitation in choosing Private Eye for one simple reason.

Private Eye is Her Majesty's favourite reading. She has a copy delivered to her bedroom every morning. It is the first paper she reads and she believes everything in it.

That is why I know that she is reading this very piece, thanking me for being so loyal by writing about her in the Mirror.

NEW OLD SAYINGS

DB/NB

SCRAPING THE BOTTOM OF THE BURRELL

I'm so loyal... I'm only selling my story to one newspaper

ONLY IN THIS WEEK'S PRIVATE EYE

Those Astonishing Paul Burrell Revelations In Full!!!

● *The Queen was a bit cold!!!*
● *Diana was a bit flaky!!!*
● *The Spencers were a bit nasty!!!*
● *Dodi was a bit Egyptian!!!*
● *I served them all soup!!!*
● *Er... That's it.*

THE WHOLE nation is asking what the hell was the Queen talking about when she warned barmy butler Burrell about "dark forces" being at work behind the scenes of our country? Did she really mean:

A "Dark forces" – secret services who were out to kill the Royal Family?

B "Dark faces" – referring to the Al-Fayed family who were out to kill the Royal Family?

C "Dark horses" – referring to 100-1 outsiders Nancy Boy and Tight Trouser in the 3.45 at Chepstow, who were out to bankrupt the Queen Mother?

D "Dark glasses" – referring to the polaroid spectacles worn as a fashion accessory by Prince William?

E "Darth Vader" – referring to the much-loved character in the Star Wars quadriology, who was out to take over the universe?

F "Clarke forces" – referring to the sinister band of Tory conspirators, who were out to kill Iain Duncan Smith and take Britain into the euro.

Phone in your answers to Boris Johnson, editor of the Spectacularlyboring. He won't be there, but you can leave a message with one of his gifted staff.

ME AND MY SPOON

RABBI BLUE

Did spoons feature in your childhood?

Hullo Brian. Hullo Sue. You know, when I was a little boy growing up in the East End of London, my old grandmother used to stir her wonderful chicken soup. One day she couldn't find the spoon. So she used a new one. And d'you know, it tasted just the same.

What's the point of this story?

Hullo Brian. Hullo Sue. The point of the story is that it isn't the spoon that gives the soup its flavour. It's what you put into it. And that's what life's like. It's what you put into it that counts. Not what you stir it with.

Can spoons play a role in reconciling different religious faiths?

Hullo Sue. Hullo Brian. There's a famous story about an old Rabbi in Poland who invited a Catholic priest to supper and found he only had one spoon. Each of them insisted that the other one used the spoon with the result that neither of them had anything to eat and they both went to bed hungry. But not together of course, because they weren't gay, like I am.

Has anything amusing ever happened to you in connection with a spoon?

I always like to see the funny side of life with spoons or anything else. It helps you get through the day. God bless, Brian. God bless, Sue.

Actually my name is Tamish.

NEXT WEEK: Ruby Wax – *"Me And My Leg Wax."*

NEW ROYAL SHOCK

There are dark forces at work

Bloody butler stole my trousers

"Kiss me and tell, Hardy"

THE SUN SAYS

Treachery of the Butler

WITH HIS decision to air Princess Diana's most intimate secrets, Paul Burrell has betrayed the Queen, Diana, the Prince of Wales, Prince William and all the Spencer family.

The culture that celebrates the villain, turning them into some sort of folk here, whilst totally forgetting the suffering of their victims must be stamped out.

But who cares? He has also committed the ultimate act of treachery.

And that, of course, is – selling his downmarket drivel to a rival paper.

We will never forget this craven act of treachery.

We say, "Burrell should rot in jail" (or ring us up with the real dirt on the gay footman – money no object).

STUDENT SHARES FLAT WITH FRIENDS SHOCK

SHOCKING news emerged last night, when it was revealed that a student will be sharing a flat with some friends.

A spokesman for the student said, "I can confirm that the rent and deposit will be split between the flatmates, whilst bills and food will remain separate."

RICH POP STAR BECOMES EVEN RICHER

A RICH pop star is set to become even richer.

MAN DOES SOMETHING TO HAIR SHOCK

IT WAS yesterday revealed that a man has done something to his hair.

One onlooker said, "It looked to me as if he'd changed his hairstyle, which would explain his slight change in appearance."

TWO LARGE TELEVISION COMPANIES MAKING RUBBISH TO BECOME ONE VERY LARGE TELEVISION COMPANY MAKING RUBBISH

(That's enough 'News'. Ed.)

GLENDA SLAGG

FLEET STREET'S 2002 NOBEL PRIZE WINNER

■ ULRIKA???! Don'tchajushate-her??? What a tramp!!? And that's puttin' it mildly, mister!!? Not content with bedding England's Swedish soccer boss, she now has to tell us all about it!! Urgh!!?! Pass the sickbag, please!!?! Take a tip from Auntie Glenda willya???! Keep your legs and your mouth shut??!?!

■ ULRIKA – hats and shoes off (geddit?!!!) to the sexy Swede who's not afraid to tell it like it is!!?! Ok, so Sven's already got a gorgeous girlfriend – who cares???! These two Scandinavian scorchers are clearly a match for each other (geddit???!). Let's leave them to it and let them feast from the smorgasbord of love in peace!???! *(This is terrible. Keep it up. Ed.)*

■ *ULRIKA – don'tchahateher???!? (You've already done this. Keep going.) Who does she think she is??!?! Edwina Currie????!!! No offence, darling, but I've seen sexier looking women working in Woolies!!!! And, as for posing in a black leather mini-skirt – ka-ka-ka-come off it, Ulrika-ka-ka!!!?!! You're a middle-aged mum, for gawd's sake!!???!! Leave the leather to hot chicks like Cherie Blair??!?!?*

■ SPARE a thought for Nancy Dell' Olio!!!?!? She's the sizzlin' Italian Signorita whose been two-timed by love rat Sven's away-from-home tactics!!?!? But is she selling her stories to the paper, telling all about her love romps???!???! *(I hope so. Ed.)* No, she is maintaining a dignified silence and appearing half-naked outside Number 10!!!! Sven, you must be completely bonkers to leave Kieron Dyer on the bench when we desperately need to shore up the left side of the English defence. *(Surely "to ditch the delicious Dell'Olio for the Stockholm strumpet"??!?!? Ed.)*

■ ULRIKA JONSSON – don'tcha-loveher? *(That is enough, even for me. Ed.)*

HERE they are, Glenda's Harvest Festival Fellas!!!?!

● **Jeremy Paxman** – How about giving this gal a hard time???!? (Geddit????!)

● **Prince Edward** – So you're not gay after all – and Ulrika says she gave you a proper job!!!?! (Geddit????!)

● **John Birt** – Not very crazy name, not very crazy guy!!?!?!

Byeeee!!!

BURRELL ON DIANA

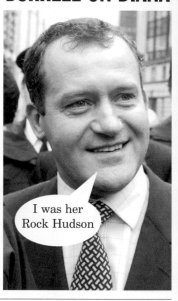

I was her Rock Hudson

HER NEW AUTOBIOGRAPHY 'ME'

MEET THE AUTHOR 6–9

SHE'S PLUGGING HER AUTOBIOGRAPHY

MAN ON TELEVISION

DIDN'T BEHAVE

DISGRACEFULLY

Shock Claim Rocks Nation

by Our TV Staff **Max Publicity**

A TELEVISION presenter faced damaging accusations yesterday that he had behaved like a normal human being. His career is thought to be on the line and TV bosses were holding urgent talks to see if he had any future in the industry. The TV presenter, whose name is well-known in media circles, was said to have enjoyed two-in-a-bed romps with his wife and to have shamelessly picked up his children from school to go on half-term and *(cont. p. 94)*

400 New Countries To Join EU by 2007

by Our European Staff **Brussel Twisk**

OVER 400 countries are soon to become members of the European Union, it was announced in Brussels last night.

Amongst the lucky winners of the Eurovision Country Contest are Slovakia, Slovenia, Slavonia, Slobodenia, Moldavia, Wallachia, Neasdonia, Tobleronia, Ulrika, Condoleeza, Nigellia, Silvikreenia, Coronia, Freedonia, Ovaltinia, Malteesia and Iraq.

Signor Romano Freebi, President of the European Com-mission, hailed this as "a new dawn for Europe, when all the countries of this great continent are finally united by their dream of being subsidised by each other".

Single European Fudge

But EU Vice-President Neil Kinnochio warned that many of the candidate countries were not yet in a position to satisfy the EU's exacting standards on fraud and corruption.

"They are not nearly corrupt enough," declared Mr Kinnochio.

DUMBLEBORE MAN DEAD

by Our Showbiz Staff **Nedwina Twinky** (17)

ONE OF the greatest actors in the Harry Potter film has died today. Richard Harris was best known for his role in the Harry Potter film where he played the Headmaster of Hogwarts, Albertus Dumble-bore, for two minutes.

Apparently, he was in some other films and used to do things in the theatre but he will always be remembered as the man with the beard in Lord of the Rings *(cont. p. 94)*

THE WORLD'S WORST COLUMNIST JOINS PRIVATE EYE!

READ TINA BROWN **today (because you won't want to next week)**

I WAS at a charity brunch at at the Hotel Miramax as the guest of Andy Brankovicz and Wolf Hackenbusch to kick around the latest big post 9/11 investment downturn. Hackenbusch was CEO of Schmooze Meldrew for 11 years (before he was ousted by überhunk Camillo Canaletto in the reverse take-over that was the talk of the Ball of the Century thrown by the Republican hostess Lily Blootz at her Long Island penthouse ranch recently valued by Snobz Magazine at a cool 3 billion dollars, making it the zazziest must-have piece of real estate this side of Oscar Snellenburger's famous Malibu beach house, where Graydon Gravadlax Jr. once memorably strutted his stuff with *(continued p.94)*

ESTELLE QUITS

I'm not up to the job

So why are you resigning?

A new leap in mobile phone technology

"Did you get the picture of me on the train?"

POETRY CORNER

In Memoriam Fritz Spiegl

So. Farewell then
Fritz Spiegl.

Musician, humorist, Impresario,
Writer and honorary
Scouser.

But you were perhaps
Best known for
The signature tune from
Z-Cars.

Da-da-da
Da-dee-dee-da-da.
Da-da-da
Di-dum-dum-dum.

> E.J. Thribb (71½)

E.J. Thribb's *Verses Against Bush's War*
can be seen on his website
www.fuckubush.com

**Lines on the discontinuance by
British Telecom of their "192"
directory enquiries service**

So. Farewell then
192.

From now on you are to be
118 500.

Or 118 118.
Or 118 119.
Or 118 000.
Or 118 811.
Or 118 888.

"Hello, this is Rajiv. What
Name is it?"

"How do you
Spell that?"

"I'm sorry, we've got
Nothing listed under that
Name."

Yes, those were your
Catchphrases.

Now we will hear them
On all the new
Numbers.

> E.J. Thribb
> (£17½ per minute)

SUPERMODELS

KERBER

JONATHAN ROSS MEETS MADONNA

JONATHAN ROSS: Fand-asdic! You look fablus! Cwoor! You look gwate! Just gwate! Darn she look fablus, laze and gennulmun? Fant-astic! Wooh! I twuly can't bleev you're here with me today! Unbleevbul! Fancy a quickie? Fant-astic! And you've also done all of us in this little countwy of ours the gwate honour of atchly coming to live amongst us!

MADONNA: Yes.

JONATHAN ROSS: Unbleevbaw. We all thank you fwom the bottom of our hearts for coming to live here. Just think of that laze and gennulmun – Madonna atchly living in England! Canyer bleev it? So er I guess you um must like it here?

MADONNA: Yes. Quite.

JONATHAN ROSS: Fand-asdic! Gwate! Thank you so much for answerwing that question! Hilawious! So now Madonna's gonna tweat us to a toadly genius new song! Let's hear it for Madonna, laze and gennulmen!

MADONNA: *Ah trahda stayur head*
Trahda stayon tarp
Trahda playapart, but somehow ahfugart
Ahdlark to spress my stream parnda vie
Ahm not chrisjun nodda jew
Ooohweeoooweeoooh
This is American Lahf.

JONATHAN ROSS: FABLUS! GWATE! FAND-ASDIC! Now, lez face it, you are the singaw biggest star in the histwy of the whirl of wall time ever. Thas quite an achievemun!

MADONNA: Wodever.

JONATHAN ROSS: Gwate! It must be litwully amazing being you! Tell us what you do on a normal day?!

MADONNA: This and that.

JONATHAN ROSS: Fand-asdic! Gwate weply! Tellyawha, if I was Madonna, I'd get out of bed, stwip naked and just look at myself in the miwwor for hours on end!!! I mean, you've got the most FANT-ASTIC physique, you weally have! Gwate bweasts! Cwooor! If I were you, I'd just go STARKERS and look at them in the miwwor all day long – then I'd turn wownd and take a gander at that incwedibull bum! Is that what you do on a normal day, then? Is it?

MADONNA: No.

JONATHAN ROSS: Gwate! Um. So,

Madonna, tell us about a day when you do somethin you weally want to do. Like, what would you do on a day when you do somethin you weally want to do – like, a day when you could do anything, so you decide to do not just anything but, like, somethin you weally want to do, f'rinstance?

MADONNA: Hmmm. A day when I do something I really wanna do. Hmmm.

JONATHAN ROSS: Yeah. I mean, like a day when you just wake up and you think, hey, I'm Madonna, I can do wodever I wanna do and what I wanna do today is to do, like, wodever I wanna do. Like, if I were you, I'd fondaw my bweasts all day, thas what I'd do! I mean, lez face it, you got twuly gwate tits, you weally have!

MADONNA: My husband and I might go to the movies. We read books. Go to a pub.

JONATHAN ROSS: Amazin! Laze and gennulmun, Madonna goes into our English pubs! Thank you so much, Madonna – you're a world superstar, but you are happy to go into an English pub! Thaz fand-asdic!

MADONNA: My husband and I go down to the Old Bull and Bush with Burlington Bertie to spend our bobs and quids on a pint of ale and eat fish and chips with brown sauce served by Pearly Kings and Queens. Chim chiminee, chim chiminee, chim-chim-cherooo. And then my husband and I jump aboard a double-decker bus and rabbit in cockney rhyming slang with Mrs Tiggywinkle and the cheery local bobbies.

JONATHAN ROSS: Fand-asdic! And do you let them feel your bweasts at all?

MADONNA: No.

JONATHAN ROSS: Shame! Ha ha ha! Let's have another bwilliand classic song. Les hearwifaw Madonna, laze and gennulmun!

MADONNA: *Doan tellmedur staaarp*
Tell the rain nodder draaarp
Tell the win nodder blo
Cos you said so
Tell meeee larvissun drew
Is jist somethin thad we do-oo-oo.

JONATHAN ROSS: Fan-dasdic! Fab-lus! We are so deeply honoured to have you among us! Now, not only do you have the most fand-asdic physique – wiwya just look at that arse, laze and gennulmun – but you are a positive GENIUS at we-invention. Like, one moment you are, like wolling naked on the sand in just a wimple, then you toadly we-invent yourself and for the next album you've toadly we-invented yourself and this time you're wolling naked on the sand – in a cowboy hat! Bwilliand!

MADONNA: I don't stick to the programme. I re-invent myself. I, like, play with the whole concept of adopting different personas as a means of, like, playing with the whole concept of different personas. By, like, reinventing myself. As a whole concept.

JONATHAN ROSS: Wight! I tell you when you looked slooply fablus – when you we-invented yourself for the vidjo for the whole Sex concept – and you were wolling naked in the sand in that littaw pill-box hat. Wowa fan-tastic body! Then before the waw in Iwaq you toadly we-invented yourself with a whole new concept in an anti-waw vidjo – wolling awound naked in the sand in a gas-mask.

MADONNA: I wanted to wake people up to the whole notion that people get hurt in wars. By appearing naked in a gas mask I wanted to say, like, people wake up, war is such a negative concept.

JONATHAN ROSS: But then you withdwew the vidjo.

MADONNA: Sure. I withdrew the video because by then the war had started, and I wanted people to, like, get behind the whole concept of war, and wake them up to the more positive notion that war could actually stop more people getting hurt.

JONATHAN ROSS: Smashin'! Fant-astic! Tellyawhat, that Guy Witchie's a lucky bloke! Fwankly, I wouldn't mind givin' you one in my dwessing woom later! Less heary for Madonna, laze and gennulmun – and the gwatest tits in the histwy of poplar music!

As told to
CRAIG BROWN

Ulrika! or Money for Old Rape

DB/△8

AZTEC NEWS

Friday 29 November 1520   3 pebbles

HORROR MASK GOES ON SHOW

by Our Art Correspondent
Quetzal Letts

A TERRIFYING human mask, dating from 2002 AD, goes on show today at the Teotihuacan Modern in Mexico City.

Said curator Hugh Montezuma-Massingberd, "This blood-curdling image will give the Aztec world a horrifying glimpse of the barbaric civilisation that is due to exist in 600 years' time."

"Jacko", the god of eternal youth and money, will be worshipped by millions of young people, some of whom will be sacrificed to him by their parents.

PYRAMID OF THE MOONWALK

He will often be depicted holding up human babies by one leg, as if he is about to dash their brains out or eat them.

The black god will also be known for his miraculous transformation into a white man.

Said Massingberd, "He is an icon of everything that this culture will symbolise – greed, excess, savagery and a lack of nose. The face of Jacko will haunt all visitors to the exhibition for years to come."

Huge queues are already forming to see what has been described as "the most frightening sight in human history".

On Other Pages

Your Mule Trains Tonight **7**

In The Cortes **6**

That Sir Alex Ferguson Citation in Full

SALUTAMUS ALEXIUS FERGUSONENSIS ALIAS 'FERGIUS' MANAGERIUS FAMOSISSIMUS MANCUNIENSIS UNITUS NATUS IN CALEDONIA IN ANNO MCMXLI SED VENIT AD MANCUNIAM ET FACTUS ARTIFEX MAXIMUS SQUADDUM PEDEBALLO DIVESISSIMUS IN MUNDO QUI VINCIT OMNES COMPETITIONES INCLUDUS PRIMERIUM LEGUM CHAMPIONORUMQUE ET FA FINALE AD STADIUM WEMBLEYENSIS NUNC FERMATUS PRO DEMOLITIONIE ET REDEVELOPMENTATIO ATQUE PROPRIETORIUS EQUUS CELERRIMUS PETRUM GIBRALTAR-IENSIS ET PUBLICAVIT LIBRUM AUTOBIOGRAPHICUM BESTSELLERENSIS SCRIPTUM AB HUGHUS MCILVANIUS HACKUS ET PISSARTICUS MAXIMUS SED SUPRA OMNES NOTABILIS QUAM PATRONUS DAVIDII BECKHAMII UXOR POSHI EX-CANTORA PUELLAE SPICORUM ET PATER BROOKLYNIS ROMEOQUE ID EST SATIS. ED.

© Universitatis Sancti Andreius (quondam North Sea Polytechnic)

Washed-Up Man On Desert Island Discs

Those IDS Choices In Full

1. *The Clarke Ascending* (*Ralph Rowan-Williams*)

2. *Ancram's Aweigh* – Band of the Royal Marines

3. *Haydn's* **194th Symphony** (the **"Very Quiet"**)

4. *Rimsky-Dunkankov's* **Symphony in John Major** (The **"Maastricht"**)

5. *Just One Portillo* (*"Arsole Mio"*) trad.

6. *On My Bike* – Normo and the Tebbs

7. *The Finished Symphony* (Schubert)

8. *Goodbyee* – Cook (Robin) and Moore (Charles)

"Listen, sunshine, I won't warn you again. 'Access' and 'Impact' are nouns, got it?!!"

Russell.

AN APOLOGY
Gordon Brown

IN COMMON with all other newspapers we may have given the impression that Mr Gordon Brown was the most capable Chancellor of the Exchequer in history, who had single-handedly put an end to the boom-and-bust disasters of former years and built up such a gigantic financial surplus that he could afford to hand out billions of pounds to schools and hospitals and still have plenty left over. Headlines such as 'Super-Gordon Does It Again', 'Cash Gordon Saves The World' and 'Brown Puts UK In The Black', may have led readers to believe that we in some way entertained the notion that Mr Brown was a financial genius of the highest order.

We now realise that Mr Brown is in fact little more than a financial nincompoop who has somehow managed to get his sums wrong to the tune of a staggering £7 billion and that his public spending plans are therefore headed for total disaster. We are happy to put the record straight and to apologise unreservedly to Mr Brown for having suggested that he had the slightest idea what he was up to.

BLAIR BLAMES AL-QAEDA FOR STORMS

by Our Weather Staff **Ulriqaeda Jonsson**

THE FIERCE storms that struck Britain last weekend could well be linked to the notorious terrorist organisation Al-Qaeda it was claimed last night.

A spokesman for the Prime Minister said, "Intelligence reports pointed to rough linkages between the 90mph gales and Osama bin Laden.

"This demonstrates beyond any shadow of a doubt," he said, "that we must invade Iraq at once."

On Other Pages

Militant Firemen: Were they trained in Afghanistan? **94**

GAY ADOPTION STORM ROCKS TORY PARTY

by Our Political Staff
John Duncan Bercough

HUMAN rights groups were in disarray last night over the vexed question of whether homosexuals should be allowed to adopt the Conservative Party.

"This is a vulnerable party," said one opponent. "What it needs is stability inside a long-term relationship – not being saddled with Michael Portillo whose lifestyle is just not suited to a committed relationship with a political party."

The unnamed spokesman continued, "Can you imagine Michael putting in the hours to nurture the Tory Party through the difficult years ahead? Of course not. He'll just flounce off at some point and make a TV documentary."

IDS Victim

But this view was denounced as "pure homophobia" by liberal critics.

"The Tory Party will be lucky to be adopted by anyone and if there is a gay person willing to take on the responsibility of looking after it, then society should be jolly well grateful."

Guy Fawkes Identity Parade

that's him

Pearsall.

TEARS AS LOST GIRL RETURNS SAFE

by Our Entire Staff **Phil Space**

THERE were scenes of undisguised grief in newspaper offices throughout Britain when a teenage girl was reported safe and sound yesterday.

As the terrible news sank in that the girl hadn't been murdered or subjected to a violent sexual assault, journalists wept openly in frustration and disappointment.

"We were looking forward to a whole month of special supplements," said one hardened hack holding back the tears, "but now we have nothing to fill up our pages."

There was a two-minute silence on the television news in the spot where they were hoping to show appeals by parents, traumatised schoolfriends, a community coming to terms with their loss and *(cont. p. 94)*

NEW SCANDAL ENGULFS BORIS SPECKER

by Our Tennis Staff **Luke O'Zade**

BLOND 38-year-old former darling of the Centre-Right Boris Specker today faced new allegations concerning his private life, when it was alleged that he had once played mixed doubles with the notorious East European-born temptress Petroushka Wyfrontikova *(cont. p. 94)*

ROYAL POETRY CORNER

That Queen's Ode in Full

Lines by Her Majesty the Queen on her departure from Castle Mae in 1997

So. Farewell
Then
Castle Mey.

With your delicious
Dinner
And your footmen
So gay.

As Queen, I
Don't often
Write in
Verse.

But I saw
Andrew Motion's
Last effort.

And thought
I couldn't do.
Much worse.

E.R. Thribb (71½)

A Taxi Driver Writes

Every week a well-known cab driver is invited to comment on an issue of topical importance.

THIS WEEK: **Johnny Prescott** (cab no. 4325)

See about them firefighters, guv? Bloody cheek, asking for 40 percent. We'd all like 40 percent, wouldn't we, guv? And for what? I'll tell yer – sitting around on their backsides playing cards and drinking cups of tea. We'd all like to do that for thirty grand. And let's face it they've all got other jobs – painters, plumbers, mini-cab drivers. What about the nurses, then? When you think how hard *they* work for peanuts. And you don't see them going on strike, do you?

Toot and support them? Bollocks! String 'em up, I say, it's the only language they understand. Oh no, I've just run into the back of a bus. Hello, hello? Emergency services? Can you get someone here quick to cut me free? No, we'd all like a 40 percent pay rise. In fact I had one last year...

SHE'S BACK! THE WORLD'S WORST COLUMNIST
TINA BROWN

THE BUZZ around the happening zone of the Upper East side is that Bloomburg's blitz bar is the new Torpedo Room, the place where you can see the likes of Rocco Schlumberger (voted top of *Forbes* Magazine's "Hottest Celebrity Orthodontists" poll) and Martha Moldstein, the ice-and-furs queen, who divorced her once-Wall Street-player husband Herman the day the Dow dived off the 68th floor and turned to jelly on the sidewalk, only for her ex to take up with Sadie Slitz, the fast-rising nymphette star of Magimix's must-see remake of *The Great Gatsby*, some of which incidentally was shot at the Long Island mansion of billionaire car rental king Luigi Clampini, whose third wife, model Vestri, features on the front cover of this month's *Glossy* Magazine, photographed by Mario Testosterone, whose stepfather, Otto Bumdorf Jr was *(cont'd. p. 94)*

Public Information Announcement

IN CASE OF FIRE, TRY NOT TO BE BURNED TO DEATH

The following tips were issued by Mr John Prescott on behalf of the government, in order to assist public safety during the firefighters' industrial action.

1. Do not get a can of petrol, spray it around the house and throw your lighted cigarette onto it.

2. Do not turn on the gas under a chip pan and go on holiday.

3. Do not give your toddler a flamethrower to play with.

4. If you are an arsonist, please try and control yourself for the duration of the emergency.

5. If you suffer from spontaneous combustion, wear an asbestos suit and stand in the garden.

6. Do not set fire to this notice.

If you require further information, visit
www.bleeding.obvious.gov.uk

FIRE KILLS
YOU CAN PREVENT IT

ME AND MY SPOON

THIS WEEK

HAROLD PINTER

Do spoons play a large part in your work?
Is that supposed to be clever? Do you get paid for asking that sort of thing?

No, what I meant was – do spoons feature in any significant way in your plays?
If you'd read any of my f*****g plays you'd know the answer to that question. I'm not going to waste my time counting up spoon references, just because you're too f*****g lazy to go to the British Library. Or why don't you go on the internet?

When you and your wife, Lady Antonia, give dinner parties...
You leave my wife out of it, you bastard. I expect you voted for f*****g Thatcher. Or are you American? I hate Americans, you're all up Bush's f*****g arse, aren't you?

May I turn now to your recent award when the Queen made you a Companion of Honour?
Are you trying to make fun of a sick man? Because if you are, I'm going to come round to your f*****g newspaper and punch you in the face, you little s**t.

Has anything amusing ever happened in your plays?
(Very long pause)

NEXT WEEK: The Aga Khan – *"Me and My Aga."*

HINDLEY STILL DEAD

by Our Crime Staff
Lunchtime O'Ghoul

THE WORLD's most evil woman is still dead.

Although it is now ten days since Myra Hindley cheated justice by dying, there are no signs that her crimes have lost their awful fascination for the editors of Britain's tabloid newspapers.

Saddleworth Moor

Today is the anniversary of the historic article I wrote yesterday, in which I gave a truly harrowing account of my visit to the bleak moors where Hindley shocked the conscience of mankind only 40 short years ago.

Words cannot express the deep sense of revulsion (continued page 94)

On Other Pages

■ Pics of dead children **10-16**

■ Pics of Hindley living life of luxury in prison **17**

■ Did Hindley kill Longford? *asks Simon Heffer* **18**

■ Should death penalty be restored for David Yelland? *asks Richard Littlejohn* **19**

■ Myra didn't fool me, says Glenda Slagg **20**

■ What is evil? *asks top philosopher Roger Screwtop* **21**

HINDLEY TO LIE IN STATE

IN RESPONSE to overwhelming public demand, the coffin of the late Myra Hindley is to lie in state in the Millennium Dome for seven days, so that members of the public will have a chance to pay their last disrespects to the most evil woman who ever lived.

Inspector Knacker, who is in charge of the arrangements for this historic national occasion, said, "We are hoping that over one million members of the public will file through the Dome in a dignified manner, to spit on the coffin or to leave a suitable tribute of cellophane-wrapped ordure."

There will also be a chance for visitors to sign a special Book of Condemnation, sponsored by the Sun newspaper, in which people can record what they would have done to Hindley if she had been let out alive.

At the four corners of the catafalque a tabloid journalist will maintain a silent vigil in honour of the woman who provided forty years' worth of voyeuristic copy for very little work *(Surely none? Ed.)*

JOIN THE TWO-MINUTE NOISE FOR MYRA

THE Sun will be marking the death of the World's Most Evil Woman with two minutes of noise. Readers all over the country are asked to join in by shouting "Rot in Hell!" (or similar sentiment) at eleven o'clock today.

Friday November 29 2002

Grauniad Obituaries

St Myra of Hindley

Myra was a witty, warm, lovable, humane, saintly woman whose embracing of the Christian faith and life of prayer were convincing proof of her genuine repentance. We at the Guardian have long championed the merits of such religious faith, well, since at least last week when it fitted in with our desire to annoy the tabloids by being ultra-liberal about someone whose beliefs we would have sneered at if she had not been a mass murderer *(cont. p. 94)*

WHY SHE WAS CREMATED

Wedding of the Century

How They Are Related

Jonathan Aitken   **Elizabeth Harris**

Jonathan The Lyingheart	The Harris of Tweed
Bad King Jonathan	Harrison Rex
Jonathan King	Robert Harris
Jeffrey The Archer	Richard Harris
Lord Beavercrook	Mata Harris
Lord Kagan	Harrison Birtwistle
Sheikh Shifti al-Bakhanda	Harrison Enfield
Jonathan The Baptist	**Dame Maria Aitken**

CLASSIC COMEDY ENDS RUN

by Our TV Staff **Simon Hefferlump**

THE CULT comedy show *The Central Office* ended its run last night, following a hilarious series of embarrassing episodes.

The show chronicled the cringe-making antics of the worst boss in the world, Iain Duncan Smith, played by actor David Brent.

Great Plots

Viewers were left in toe-curling agony when in the final instalment IDS was sacked and begged for his job back.

This followed his dire attempt to become a motivational speaker and his dismal efforts to tell jokes. Critics feel that the comedy cannot possibly get any better and that *The Central Office* should now stop for good.

Great Tory

Viewers, however, love the show and have begged the producers for more of IDS's excruciating exploits.

But with a new boss in charge would *The Central Office* ever be the same again?

Daily Cawdorgraph

1 groat

DOUBTS GROW OVER FIRST LADY

by Our Man at Number Thane *William Deedespeare*

THERE was mounting concern last night over the influence exercised by Lady Macbeth on her husband.

Unconfirmed reports have linked her name with a group of unsavoury characters, some of whom she has introduced to King McBlair.

Is This A Whopper I see Before Me?

They are said to include a group of three "lifestyle gurus" who have been trying to market a new slimming potion made from organic materials, including eyes of newt, spleen of toad and wing of bat.

One of the advisers claims that she can get in touch with the spirit world and there are even reports that seances have been held where the ghosts of the dead (Gordon Brownquo) have materialised.

Out out out

A spokesman for Lady McBlair told reporters, "The First Lady suffers from insomnia and needs help from professional sleep therapists. One of the proposed remedies to restore her mental balance is to go and wash her hands all the time."

Meanwhile, Alastair Campbell, the chief of the McSpin clan and a personal friend of King Macbeth's, has tried to distance the Scottish ruler from his wife's personal concerns.

"Lady McBlair is an independent career woman," he said, "and who she murders is entirely her own affair."

ON OTHER PAGES

"And another thing, that lifestyle guru of yours is a bloody waste of money"

HONEYSETT

CHERIE IN PROPERTY SCANDAL

I've got a nice pair of Bristols

Mine are flats

THE CONMAN WHO FOOLED CHERIE BLAIR

by Our Political Staff **Peter Foster**

A KNOWN conman with a long history of duping the public has become dangerously close to Cherie Blair, it has been revealed.

The confidence trickster, who goes by the name of Tony Blair (sometimes "the Prime Minister") befriended Cherie Blair and managed to convince her that he was a member of the Labour Party.

In fact, Tony was simply a hustler on the make, using Cherie's connections to further his career. He is not wanted in a number of countries apart from Britain and is the author of numerous failed scams including health, education and public transport.

"He is so believable," said one innocent victim. "He promises you the earth and then a few months later you realise you've been had."

Said another, Mr G. Brown, of Downing Street, "The man's a scoundrel. He told me that I could be Prime Minister. I feel a mug for being taken in so easily."

However, a spokesman for Cherie Blair issued a denial: "Mrs Blair has only met Tony once, at their wedding, and does not rely on him for any advice, financial or otherwise."

COURT CIRCULAR

10, DOWNING STREET

Tuesday: HM the Prime Minister and HRH Princess Cherie received the President of Syria and Mrs Assad at a State Banquet. The Princess was attended by the Mistress of the Shower, Ms Carole Crackpot and Dowager Mistress of the Healing Oils, Mrs Sylvie Crackpot. Mr Peter Frodster faxed over apologies for his absence.

Wednesday: HM the Prime Minister and HRH Princess Cherie gave a luncheon in honour of the editor of the Sun newspaper, Sir David Yelland and his wife Lady Leylandii Yelland. Also present was the Master of the Spin, Sir Alastair Campbell of that Lie, attended by his live-in partner Dame Fiona Millbank. They were later joined by HRH Prince Euan who had been on a Royal tour of various local hostelries.

In the evening the Princess Cherie presented the awards at a charitable function, whcre she made a speech on behalf of Amnesiacs Anonymous.

I'm a part-time judge of character

Thursday: Lord Booth of Scousegit continued his provincial tour, with a visit to the bookselling establishment of Messrs Waterstone in Kingston-on-Hull, where he signed three copies of his memoirs *A Portrait of the Piss Artist As An Old Man*.

HRH the Princess Lauren of Booth graciously contributed yet another article about her sister to the periodical *The New Statesman* *(That's enough Court Circular. Ed.)*

ME AND MY SPOON

THIS WEEK

CAROLE CAPLIN

What part do spoons play in your holistic healing therapy?

I believe that anything that is made of metal can be used as a conduit for energy that drives out toxins. If you hold up a spoon pointing to the magnetic meridian of the body, then a qualified healer, such as myself, can literally cure almost any disease you can think of.

Did you give the prime minister's wife a spoon massage?

My dealings with Cherie are totally confidential. She is a very close personal friend, as is the prime minister, so I cannot possibly comment on that question. But the answer is yes, I've frequently given both of them spoon therapy as part of an Aztec rebirthing ritual. They both loved it, and said afterwards that it had done wonders for their sex life. But more than that I cannot say.

I understand your boyfriend Peter Foster has stolen a number of your spoons. Is that true?

Peter is a lovely man and I am sure, if he did steal my spoons, he had a very good reason for doing so, like he wanted to sell them.

Has anything amusing ever happened to you in connection with a spoon?

I am getting paid for this, aren't I? I'm fed up with the media trying to exploit my private life. So let's call it 50 grand, shall we?

NEXT WEEK: Michael Fish – *"Me and My Fish."*

COUGH'S BOGUS CV SHOCK

by Our Political Staff **Francis Wheeze**

IN AN amazing revelation last night, Mr Iain Duncan Cough was found to have lied on his curriculum vitae.

Amongst his various qualifications and job descriptions in the latest edition of *Who's He*, Duncan Cough claims that he is currently "the leader of the Conservative Party".

After a detailed investigation by reporters lasting several minutes, it has become clear that this is "a complete fabrication".

Said one expert, "He may well have been to meetings in Smith Square and certainly people have seen him in the building, but to say that he is leader is laughable."

Mr Duncan Cough buried his lie amidst a list of more credible details of his career, such as his degree in Astrophysics from the University of the Moon (formerly Sea of Tranquility Polytechnic), his doctorate in brain surgery from Oxford College, Cambridge and his best-selling novels including "Kane and Abel", "Not a Penny More" and "First Among Equals".

Exclusive to Private Eye

That Fayed Sunday Telegraph Letter

Before Editing	**What You Actually Read**
You Fuggin' Lawson, You fuggin' shut up you shiddy-face with your shiddy wife, you try and fuggin' make out I'm some kinda fuggin' crook well the fuggin' laugh is on you innit you shiddy-faced fugger. Who's got the biggest fuggin' dick now?	Dear Sir, For the past few years, this newspaper has used its columns to write about me in a consistently negative and critical way *(continues for 94 pages)*

SOMEONE TELLS TRUTH SHOCK

by Our Media Staff

SOMEBODY IN public life told what appeared to be the truth.

He immediately apologised, telling reports, "I don't know what came over me. I just blurted it out without thinking."

Asked if he was going to resign on the grounds that he was unfit to hold office he said, "You're right. I have let everyone down, my colleagues, my family and myself." He added "My wife is not standing by me at this difficult time and I deserve everything that happens to me."

What do you think should happen to the man who told the truth?

Join the Eye's interactive poll and you decide how high he should be strung up!

Email:onlylanguagetheyunderstand@cab-driver.con

"Can I have some whelks, please?"

CHRISTMAS GIFTS

From The Great House Of Windsor Sale

brian bagnall

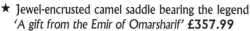

Make it a Christmas to remember with a special Royal Gift for your loved ones. Look at these amazing offers.

★ Jewel-encrusted camel saddle bearing the legend *'A gift from the Emir of Omarsharif'* **£357.99**

★ Silver-plated monkey wrench inscribed *'To Charles and Diana from the loyal people of Huddersfield'* **£25 (ono)**

★ An after-dinner mint presented to Prince Charles on the occasion of the Royal Jubilee Dinner at the Ritz **£19.33**

★ Set of audiotapes detailing a series of unnatural acts performed by various members of Prince Charles' staff **£1.3 million**

And there's much, much more in this incredible Christmas bonanza from the House of Windsor – cheap is our middle name!!

Hurry, hurry, hurry whilst Royal Family lasts!

CHRISTMAS TV

The Conman

RONNIE BIGGS's immortal and much-loved Christmas classic in which little Cherie looks out of the window and sees the Conman come to life. Before she knows what has happened, he has whisked her off onto the front pages of all the newspapers. But when the Sun comes out (and the Daily Mail as well) the Conman melts away, leaving Cherie in tears.

Includes Aled Jones's unforgettable rendition of "We're Taking in The Blairs".

*ALSO
Pyscho II

RE-MAKE of Hitchcock horror-classic complete with even more spine-chilling version of 'that shower scene', when looney Caroline Caplin attacks innocent Cherie Blair with an organic loofah. "The sight of Cherie's toxins dribbling away down the plug-hole remains a cinema classic," says TV's Barry Norman.

Rudolf The Red-Brick Reindeer

EXCLUSIVE
CHERIE BLAIR on GERMAINE GREER

Haven't we all had enough of this screaming, wild-eyed woman ranting on all over the place?

As a feminist, I *(cont'd. p. 94)*

NATIVITY AUDITIONS

ME! ME! ME!

grizelda

"They all want to play the star"

POLLY FILLER

Author of the Best-Selling 'Mummy For Old Rope'

CHRISTMAS is always the most magical time of year – falling snow, children skating and the coloured lights twinkling in Macy's window. It's just a shame my family won't be here in New York to celebrate with me. But it wasn't practical, given my hectic schedule of book promotion with interviews, personal appearances and the odd bit of shopping to relax. Of course I feel guilty – don't all working mums walking the tightrope of their careers? But, as ever, I have somehow pulled off the balancing act by hiring an extra au pair for Christmas (delightful Ugandan girl who tells us the average wage there is 20p a day. No wonder she is so thrilled when I pay her 25p!).

So the useless Simon and his two little helpers will have to play Santa this year and do something for once, instead of watching Celebrity Goose-Eating on BBC Digital's No One's Watching Channel, presented by Jeremy Vine.

OVER here in the Big Apple you'll be pleased to know that New York has rolled out the red carpet and embraced me as a daughter. Everyone in the United States has gone Polly Filler mad! From Mexican cab drivers to Korean bellboys, there is only one topic of conversation and that is my best-selling new novel *Mummy For Old Rope*. And the word from Tinseltown is that all of Hollywood's top actresses are queuing up to play me! Jennifer Lopez, Penelope Cruz and Catherine Zeta Jones have all put themselves forward, saying "I am Polly Filler. This is the hilarious but emotional story of my life too. I'll do it for nothing, it's so brilliant."

Unfortunately, they are all too fat and old to quite capture the real me – juggling the roles of mother and best-selling author of *Mummy For Old Rope*.

Also, I am not sure that any of these actresses are up to playing me in the heartrending Christmas climax of the book where the guilt-ridden Polly has to go on a book promotion tour rather than spend vital quality time with her beloved toddler. It's a classic Polly Filler moment when our heroine manages to bring a Christmas smile to her toddler's face when she picture messages a photo of herself having lunch with Steven Spielberg.

In the end, I think there's only one person good enough to play me. And that's myself!

As it says in my best-selling book *Mummy For Old Rope*, Polly Christmas and a Filler New Year!

© *Polly Filler*

New from Gnometel

CHARLOTTE CHURCH

VOICE OF AN ANGEL

Charlotte "Voice of an Angel" Church sings all your traditional Christmas favourites

INCLUDING:

- Ding Dong Merrily on the Aeroplane
- Oh Come All Ye Faithful (But not to Meet and Greet)
- The Hello! and the I've-Got-Boyfriend
- F*** You Merry Gentlemen
- Silent Night (Concert Cancelled)

HURRY, HURRY – WHILST SHOCKS LAST!

THE TIMES

LONDON 1863–1970

MR GILBERT'S WIDOW TO SUE SIR ARTHUR SULLIVAN

by Our Special Correspondents Mr Lennon and Mr McCartney

Sir Arthur Sullivan, the nation's most respected composer, has had a setback in his campaign to have the name of his partnership altered from the familiar "Gilbert and Sullivan" to "Sullivan and Gilbert".

Mr Gilbert's widow, Nanki Poo, has embarked on legal proceedings to restrain Sir Arthur, claiming that the success of the famous Savoy operas was due entirely to her late husband's genius. Sir Arthur, she told The Times, was "no more than a mediocre banjo-player who merely thought up a few tunes to go with my husband's immortal words".

"Yes, I'd like to complain about next door's bird table"

THEN AND NOW

1. Mirror bully accused of financial impropriety, investigated by DTI, uses newspaper to try and discredit Private Eye.

2. Ends up falling off yacht.

1. Mirror bully accused of financial impropriety, investigated by DTI, uses newspaper to try and discredit Private Eye.

2. Er...

BRITISH COCAINE AWARDS

by Our Special Correspondent **Jon Snow**

A GLITTERING line-up of stars from the world of cocaine gathered last night for the industry's biggest night of the year.

A showbiz expert said, "These awards are very significant, as they usually determine who will develop the costliest habit over the next twelve months – once again, standards were very high this year, but there again, not nearly as high as some of the nominees."

Stop Press

Man Arrested For Telling Joke In Toilet

GLENDA SLAGG

FLEET STREET'S MISS WORD (GEDDIT???)

■ MISS WORLD??!?! Miss Third World more like!! Well, I'm going to give it a miss??! (Geddit???!) Who needs this meat market of scantily-dressed flesh for dirty old men to sit around a-leerin' and a-sneerin'??!? The whole thing stinks!!? No wonder the muslims of Nigeria showed their distaste by burning down churches and murdering everyone?!?! Hats off to them for showing commonsense and trying to bring the world into the 21st century!!?!?!

■ HATS and bikinis off to the plucky contestants of Miss World!!?!! They weren't going to be cowed by a bunch of mad muslims a-shootin' and a-lootin'!!?!?! These gals stood firm (Geddit!!?!) as they showed what us girls can do to make the world a better place and stop the fun-killing fundamentalists (Geddit??!) from dragging us back into the Middle Ages!!?!?! I wouldn't **miss** it for the world!!?!?!

■ *THREE CHEERS for plucky Princess Anne, the only Royal who had the guts to stand up in court and take her punishment!!? Unlike* her gutless brother Charles who preferred to skulk behind Mummy's petticoats whilst Royal Butler Paul Burrell was thrown to the **dogs**!?!?! (Geddit???!) The Princess Royal stood in the dock noble, dignified and guilty. God bless you, Ma'am!??!

■ PRINCESS ANNE – £500??!? What kind of fine is that for a woman whose dog ate a toddler??!? What kind of justice is that???! The Princess should have been put down – along with her dotty dog!?!? As I always say, "It's one law for the bitch..."!?!?! (Geddit???)

HERE they are, Glenda's Yuletide Yummies!!!?!

● **Daniel Deronda** – OK, so he's fictional but so's my sex life!?!

● **Andrew Marr** – They call him Big Ears!!?! I wonder what else is big??!? Geddit!?!?!

● **Andy Gilchrist, General Secretary of the Fire Brigades' Union** – I've got a fire that needs quenchin' Big Boy – so bring your hose round. Geddit!!?!?!

Byeeee!!!

MASSACRE OF INNOCENTS 'A SYSTEM FAILURE' Says Inquiry

BY OUR CURRENT AFFAIRS STAFF FRANK INCENSED

A REPORT into the death of all children under the age of one in the Judean region has concluded that "a lack of communication" between departments in the Social Services was the main cause of the tragedy.

A spokesman for the Inquiry said, "Social Services and local health workers may have been alerted to the nature of King Herod and it is certainly true that he gave some indication of homicidal tendencies throughout his reign. When he issued an edict that all of the firstborn of the land were to be slaughtered there is an argument to say that the relevant authorities should have been aware of it and should have acted in some way. But the Inquiry has found that no one was to blame, apart from the system itself."

He concluded, "It is all very sad, but rest assured it will never happen again."

Harrods sale

This way to the bedding department

You'll be fuggin' lucky

The Times Friday January 10 2003

LETTERS TO THE EDITOR
Popular First Names
From Lady Fantonia Pinter

Sir, As is customary at this time of year, I am sending you a list of the most popular names for boys and girls in the year 2002, based on announcements in your Births column.

BOYS	GIRLS
1 Osama	1 Edwina
2 Dubya	2 Condoleezza
3 Rumsfeld	3 Kylie
4 Romeo	4 Camilla
5 Aragorn, son of Arathorn	5 Mugabe
6 Dumbledore	6 Galadriel
7 Sven	7 Cherie
8 Saddam	8 Carole
9 Enron	9 Dame Judy
10 The Earl of Onslow	10 Sex and the City

Yours faithfully,
LADY FANTONIA PINTER,
Dunhomecomin, London W11.

"You think you're so clever, don't you, Brian!?!!"

Not Only Another Programme About Peter Cook But Also One Featuring All The Same People Who Were In All The Others (BBC1, Holiday Friday)

This was the 54th documentary about Peter Cook broadcast in the past year, but only the seventh last week. Highlights included some old men who knew him at Cambridge, some slightly younger men who met him in London and some even younger men who saw him on TV in the last years of his life and thought he was very funny. Perhaps best summed up by the great Dr Sir Jonathan Miller, when he compared Cook's "cracking of the comedic code" with Harvey's discovery of the circulation of the blood and (Continued p. 94)

That Honorary Degree Citation in Full

SALUTAMUS BRIANUS MAIAM, GUITARISTUM PRINCIPALIS IN 'REGINA', GROUPUS POPULARIS CANTORIBUS, FAMOSISSIMUS PER 'RHAPSODIA BOHEMIENSIS' CUM FREDERICUS MERCURIENSIS (EHEU NUNC MORTUUS), SED ATQUE FAMOSUS PER PERFORMANS SUPER PALACIO BUCKINGHAMENSIS CUM INSTRUMENTUM ELECTRONICUM IN CELEBRATIONE JUBILATIONE AUREUM BRENDA REGINA IN ANNO MMII ET EXPERTUS IN ARTE ASTRONOMICA ET AMATOR PUELLAE ANITA DOBSONENSIS QUONDAM STELLA IN SAPONA OPERA EASTENDIBUS NOMINE ANGIA ET... ER... ID EST.

© The University of Hertfordshire (formerly Baldock Little Chef)

BLUNKETT LEADS NUMERACY DRIVE

Introducing

Max Hastings

The World's Worst Columnist

Why We Should Get Up In The Mornings

IT'S all too easy, isn't it, to wake up in the morning and think, "Oh stuff it, I'm going to turn over and go back to sleep." When the choice is between the snug warmth of the bedclothes and the bracing chill of a dark winter morning, nine times out of ten one's inclination is to stay put.

And why not? Recent polls have shown that many of you share my feelings about the difficulty of getting up in the morning. It is one of the hardest things most of us have to do in the entire day.

Wasn't it P.G. Wodehouse (or was it Winston Churchill?) who said "Early to bed, early to rise, is not a good idea"?

Keep Going, P.D.

But what is the alternative? Wouldn't the nation quickly grind to a halt if we all decided to stay in bed?

Just think about it for a minute. No trains. No buses. No smiling postman to push our letters through the door.

A grim prospect indeed. And one which reinforces my long-held view that it is desirable for the good of the community that all of us who are capable of doing so should make the effort and get out of bed.

And anyway, once you're up, it's not really half as grim as you think it's going to be.

Once you've gritted your teeth, slung your legs over the side of the bed, found your glasses and pulled on an old dressing gown, the world doesn't seem too bad a place after all!

Particularly when your slumbers have been interrupted by a call from the editor of the Daily Mail offering you £5000 for writing a load of drivel like this.

© Hastingstrash Productions.

Great Education Policies No. 94

"By cancelling maths we'll save... nearly got it... three... no, two hours... hang on..."

LORD JENKINS CLARET POURS IN

(Surely 'Tributes'? Ed.)

by Our Staff **Lunchtime O'Bituary**

TRIBUTES poured in today to the man they called the giant of modern politics.

Reformer, statesman, political biographer, and the creator of New Labour, he will be remembered above all for his gift for claret *(Surely "friendship"? Ed.)*

Britain's most senior politicians yesterday queued up to pay their respects to this "middle of the road" colossus.

The Prime Minister **Tony Blair** said, "He was a great man whose greatest achievement was to destroy the Labour Party, thus making it possible for someone even greater than him to take it over."

Said **Lord Healey**, "People say he was the greatest Prime Minister Britain never had. How wrong they are. I can think of at least one former Labour Chancellor with much bushier eyebrows who would have been a much better Prime Minister than him."

Said **Roy Hattersley**, "We may have had our differences, but we were both called Roy and we both enjoyed a good lunch."

Said **Lord Harris of Kintbury**, "I well remember him saying over one of our lunches at the Old Boar at Snorebury that we must have another lunch again soon."

Said **David Owen**, "Roy's greatest and indeed only talent was writing books and even then he wasn't much good. We will never see his like again, fortunately."

Said **Mrs Margaret Thresher**, of the East Hendred Branch of the Wine-To-Snack conglomerate, "This is a sad day for the world of claret. Lord Jenkins was one of the great political drinkers of our time who broke the mould from the Stilton at Christmas to accompany an excellent bottle of chateau *(cont. p. 94)*

LORD JENKINS OF HILLHEAD
1920-2003
WIP

McLACHLAN

BLUNKETT ATTACKS GOD

by Our Religious Staff
Archbishop Rowan Pelling

THE Home Secretary hit out this week at "the bearded old lefty sitting on a cloud, completely out of touch with everyday concerns".

Said Mr Blunkett, writing in *Beards and Beardmen* (formerly the *Spectator*), "His language is impenetrable and no one has any idea what he is trying to say. What I take to be his criticism of this government is completely wrong. He should keep out of politics and concentrate on what he does best, ie moving in a mysterious way."

Yesterday, God would make no comment.

BLAIR TO CRACK DOWN ON 'REPLICA GUNS'

by Our Firearms Staff **Phil Withsand**

THE Government has ordered an immediate inquiry into the number of "replica guns" which are being used by the British Army.

The weapons look like real guns but, in the event of an armed conflict, immediately jam and fail to fire.

"It's a disgrace," said the Prime Minister. "All these criminals have got guns that actually work, whilst our lads in the Gulf have got these duds.

"Something must be done, but not, obviously, by me."

KIDS STUFF
NEW! COMBINED GUN AND MOBILE PHONE

RSJ

School news

St Cakes

Gun term begins today. There are 432 dead in the school and several wounded. P.J. Kalashnikov (Shooters) is Keeper of the Arsenal. A.K. Uzi (Sawnoffs) is Captain of Drive-bys. The Head of Music, Rev. J.S. Vaughan-Williams, has been replaced by Mr "Bo" P. Diddy Deadboy, formerly Head of Music in Rampton High Security Prison. There will be a performance of "Bonny and Clyde" (adapted for the street by Mr Deadboy) on 7th March, St Armalite's Day. Crossfires will be held on the killing fields on 12th February. Raps will be granted on April 2nd.

WAS ROY JENKINS THE MOST EVIL MAN WHO EVER LIVED? Asks Peter Hitchens

FOR 30 years a tidal wave of permissive filth and violence has swept over our once-proud nation.

Today Britain is a country where crack dealers openly gun each other down in the streets, where teenage mothers have abortions on their way to school, where prisoners in their cells are allowed to download child porn under the Human Rights Act, where asylum seekers are given lottery grants to manufacture deadly poison gas, and where giant rats emerge from the sewers every night to gnaw at the corpses of 10-year-old children who have been forced into prostitution by Albanian yardies.

And who is responsible for every detail of this horrifying slide into the slime of our modern decadence?

Step forward, Royston Cadwallader Jenkins, the hero of the chattering classes, with his plummy voice, his Garrick Club manners, his claret-swilling bonhomie and his lifelong love of the European Union.

It was this man who, when Home Secretary, single-handedly destroyed everything that Britain had stood for through the centuries. It was his 1967 Abolition Of All That Britain Has Stood For Down The Centuries Act which opened the floodgates to *(cont. p. 94)*

You can now read a fuller version of this article on Peter Hitchens' own website at www.hitchbonkers.loonie.com

HOW THE SUN WILL CHANGE UNDER A WOMAN

OUT GOES

Saucy page 3 photos of luvvlies

IN COMES

Raunchy page 3 pics of naked totty (plus some on the front page as well)

OUT GOES

Prurient sex-obsessed celebrity drivel

IN COMES

Bonking stories about telly stars

OUT GOES

Slavish support for whoever is in power

IN COMES

Robust adulation for whoever looks most popular

OUT GOES

Taxi driver's view of world

IN COMES

White van man's grasp of international affairs
(That's enough Ed.)

NEW EDITOR FOR SUN

Yes, it's me again!

WHAT YOU WON'T SEE IN THE SUN

PAGE 3 STUNNA!

WHAT A "WAPPING PAIR" – Rebekah and the Sun, that is! She is the new Editphwoar of Britain's top Nudespaper – and we can't Wade for her to show us a woman's view!! She always wanted to reveal things – well, how about this Rebekorr! But don't feast your eyes on this raunchy Red-Top too long fellas – or you could be named and shamed! No wonder she got a rise out of Rupert!! He hasn't made a boob this time (continued in witless vein forever)

"I'm going to be late, I'm having a bad nose hair day"

IRAQ: INSPECTORS MAKE SENSATIONAL DISCOVERY

by Our Man In Baghdad SARAH SANDS

THE UNITED Nations weapons inspectors today reported "an incredible find" that makes war inevitable.

Smoking Barrell

The discovery of a huge quantity of oil buried deep under the desert is sure to prompt military intervention.

Washington hawks were jubilant at the find. Said General H.J. Kickassburger, "Saddam thought he could hide it. But now we know he is sitting on vast stockpiles of WMD (Wells of Major Dimensions). Now we can send in the tankers."

MOTION POEM ENDS WAR
Peace Breaks Out

by Our Poetry Staff Tom Appaulin

THE PRESIDENT of the United States today announced an astonishing u-turn after reading the Poet Laureate's poem, *'Causa Belli'*.

President Bush told a shocked news conference, "Until I read these lines I had no idea that war was not very nice. Now I realise that the whole thing has been a terrible mistake."

The President then called off the war and instead of a task force, sent a copy of the poem to Saddam Hussein.

"I am sure that once Saddam has seen this," he said, "he will never do anything nasty ever again."

That Poem In Full

They read good books,
But not my verse,
If only they did,
Things wouldn't get any worse.

A Taxi Driver Writes

Every week a well-known cab driver is invited to comment on an issue of topical importance.

THIS WEEK: **John Le Cabbie** on "The War With Iraq"

Blimey. Them Yanks have all gone mad, haven't they, guv? I mean, Bush is clean off his rocker, i'n't he? He's just like a cowboy. As for that Rumpole and Congerella, all they're after is Saddam's oil, innit? It's obvious. You know what I'd do with that bunch of lunatics? I'd have 'em all on Death Row and give 'em a taste of their own medicine. That'd teach 'em. I 'ad that Allan Greenspan in the back of my cab once. Very clever man.

NEXT WEEK: Borrie Johnson on "Why I never go to the House of Commons".

"Strange... I've just had a text message... it says 'Lying in dark, small place – where the hell am I?'"

IN THE COURTS

Cleese v. The Evening Standard Day 94

Before Mr Justice Cocklecarrot

Sir Ephraim Hugefee Q.C. *(for the plaintiff Mr John Cleese)*: When my client read the report in the Evening Standard alleging that he had lost his sense of humour, he flew into a tantrum and shouted, "I do not see anything funny about that. I shall sue!"

(The court was told that the Evening Standard had apologised for what Mr Cleese had claimed was "the most outrageous slur ever perpetrated on a distinguished public servant in the history of libel". The newspaper had also offered the sum of £10,000 as compensation for his "hurt feelings". Mr Cleese himself then gave evidence via a special video link from Los Angeles.)

Mr Cleese: Hallo there, Your Honour. I'm sorry I can't be with you all on this special day, but I am very famous and rich and can't be bothered to come back to England just for some silly court case.

Mr Justice Cocklecarrot: I am indebted to you, Mr Cleese, as indeed is the whole world, for your wonderful contribution to comedy. My wife in particular especially enjoyed your celebrated Basil Python...

Cleese: It's 'Fawlty', My Lord.

Judge: Then perhaps the usher would be good enough to adjust the set!

(Sycophantic laughter from assembled QCs)

Hugefee: Sir Jonathan, will you tell the court what your feelings were when you read this vile calumny upon your person in Miss Waddilove's newspaper?

Cleese: My first feeling was one of shock and outrage that such a thing could be written and published about someone as important as myself. But this gave way to feelings of acute depression, and I ended in genuine fear for my life.

(The witness here broke down in tears.)

Cocklecarrot: Perhaps you would like a brief adjournment to recover by taking a swim in that agreeable pool I see behind you.

Cleese: I am indebted to you, Your Lordship.

Cocklecarrot: No, as I said before, Mr Cleese, it is we who are indebted to you, for The Full Monty Python and that wonderful series you did about the Germans during the war.

Cleese: It is not the money that bothers me, Your Honour. It is the fact that they didn't offer me enough of it!

Cocklecarrot: That is highly amusing and, I would suggest, prima facie evidence that you have not, as the defendants alleged, lost your sense of humour!

(QCs erupt into paroxysms of hysterical mirth at judicial wit. The judge reserved judgement for several weeks to give him time to retire to the Garrick Club for luncheon.)

"What do you reckon? Launch an initiative, set a target... or actually do something?"

Yes! It's The Possible Marital Break-Up Of The Century!!

How They Are Still Related

(at time of going to press)

Zoe Ball

Lucille Ball
|
Terry Major-Ball
|
Alan Ball
|
Zoe Wannamaker
|
Zoe Heller
|
Ed Balls
|
Zola Budd

Fatboy Slim

Field Marshal Slim
|
Fats Domino
|
Boy George
|
George Melly
|
Fats Waller
|
Fats Soames
|
Fat Roy Jenkins

NEW PUBLIC TOILET LAW REFORM

by Our Legal Affairs Staff **W.C. 'Dirty' Deedes**

FROM tomorrow the act of going to the toilet in a public lavatory will be against the law.

Hilary Benny Hill

The government has announced a wide-ranging review of legislation aimed at "cleaning up" public behaviour in order to ensure that innocent people having sex in public conveniences will no longer have to be embarrassed by a minority of irresponsible individuals who seek to use the facilities in order to go to the toilet.

Said a spokesman, "As war looms and the economy crashes, the government has rightly decided to crack down on this filthy habit of bowel evacuation in places where ordinary cottaging homosexuals are trying to go about their business."

The Homosexual Office

He continued, "If members of the public wish to relieve themselves, they should obviously go in the privacy of their own gardens or possibly in their cars, but not, of course, with the curtains open."

SHUT THE FUCK DOWN!

Quentin Tarantino logs off

TUNNEL OF CELEBRITY LOVE

HUNTer

Notes & Queries

QUESTION: Who invented the clothes peg?

☐ CONTRARY to the ludicrous and long-discredited theory put forward by the Rev. Titchmarsh, the clothes peg was never used in Chinese religious ceremonies during the Pong dynasty (404-312 BC). The first authenticated record of the clothes peg dates back only to the second half of the 17th century, when this useful device was invented by the German mathematician Klaus von Pegg. Pegg observed that washing hung over rope 'lines' in the courtyard of his lodging house in Mannheim was often caught by gusts of wind and blown into the nearby River Schmaltz. In his efforts to make the washing more secure, Herr Pegg first attempted to fasten it to the line with a glue based on goose fat and rye flour (goseglaü). But this had the disadvantage that the clothes had to be rewashed to remove the glue. Eventually, after many further experiments over a period of 30 years, Herr Pegg came up with the device which has taken his name. He originally constructed these from branches of a hidden tree cut from the churchyard of the famous Jakobskirke. Readers wishing to know more should consult my own work "The Father Of The Modern Clothes Peg", published by the Rusbridger Press in 1973. J. Pegg (Dr), Winnipeg, Ontario.

Question: What is the origin of the popular surname 'Stothard'?

☐ THE name derives from Anglo-Saxon, being a corruption of the original word "Stoat-herd". It was customary in the early mediaeval period to keep flocks of stoats which were much prized for their skill in locating wild mandrakes, which were a delicacy when roasted with apples. The person assigned to guard the stoats was usually a simple fellow who could be relied upon to do whatever his master told him. The stoatherd was often jokingly referred to as "Sir Stoatherd", as in Shakespeare's Midsummer's Night Dream (III, ii):

Fool: *Why, Sir Stoatherd, what nonsense thou hast writ in thy newspaper.*

Yours truly, Professor Anwar Radjuit, University of Bangalore.

Answers, please, to the following: a) Why do bees hum? b) Can fish see in colour? c) Why hasn't Taki been sacked from the Spectator?

From the pen that brought you *Heir of Sorrows, La Dame Aux Camillas* and *Born To Be Queen*, comes a special love story for Valentine's Day

NEVER TOO OLD

by Dame Sylvie Krin

THE STORY SO FAR: Multi-billionaire media mogul Rupert Murdoch has married a fragrant young oriental beauty from the land of birds nest soup.

Now read on...

"I GOT great news for you, Lupert," purred the lovely Wendy Deng, as she entered the gymnasium of their 48th storey Manhattan penthouse apartment.

"You mean you're going to switch off this bloody rowing contraption and give me an ice-cold tinnie?" puffed the sweating septuagenarian tycoon, as he tried to keep up with the machine's remorseless demands.

"First guess wrong," hissed his peach-skinned paramour, as she turned up the machine to 'Olympic Standard (Bronze) Level'.

"You mean, we've got the Sky Shopping Channel into Tibet?" he guessed with a wan smile, as golf-balls of sweat rolled off the walnut wrinkles of his fast-ageing face. "Brilliant!"

"Wrong again, Lupert, you pretty dim sum for billionaire magnate."

"Steady on, sheila."

"My name Wendy, you silly old man. No, you remember what you were doing three months ago, that night in Kowloon Ramada Honeymoon Suite?"

Suddenly it all came back to him.

The velvet of the tropical night. The musak in the lift playing John Lennon's *Imagine*. The amber liquid flowing like water – cripes, he'd had a skinful that night.

And what was that stuff she'd put in his cocoa? Powdered rhino horn, she'd said – "ancient Chinese herbal remedy to put smile on face of tired old man".

Blimey, so that's what she was on about, he thought.

"Jeez, you don't mean you're up the duff again? You've only just popped one out. You'd think I was only firing blanks at my age."

"No, no," soothed the Manchurian mother-to-be from the land of crispy duck with plum sauce and pancakes, "you super-fertile hunky big boy. You number one jig-a-jig."

Letting go of the oars, he slumped forward on the machine and buried his head in his hands.

"God Almighty, Wend," he croaked. "You know what this is going to mean? More waking up at 3 in the morning. More sleepless nights. More pushing the buggy round Central Park. More of the little buggers climbing all over me when I'm trying to catch 40 winks between global video conferences."

He searched her doll-like porcelain visage for a trace of compassion. "You know what this will do to me, Wend, don't you? It'll kill me."

An inscrutable smile flickered across her cherry-red lips, as she turned the machine up to 'Steve Redgrave – Danger Level'.

Outside, black clouds were rolling up over the Manhattan skyline, plunging the city into night.

© *World copyright Sylvietrash Productions, in collaboration with The Gatwick Airport Collection.*

THOMAS THE PRIVATISED TANK ENGINE

BY THE REV. TAWDRY

ALL the engines were lined up to hear the Fat Controller's new idea. They were all looking worried.

"I have some good news," he said proudly. "From now on none of you will be late again."

Thomas was very pleased because he and his friends hated being late and upsetting the passengers.

"How will you do that?" asked Henry, cheekily.

"Simple," said the Fat Idiot (*Surely "Controller"? Rev. A.*)

"I'm going to cancel you all, so then none of you can be late ever again."

"Hoorah!" shouted no one.

© The Rev. Tawdry 2003

NEXT WEEK: The adventures of Ron The Replacement Bus Service.

'CELEBRITY NOT PAEDOPHILE' SHOCK

by Our Crime Staff P.D. O'TOWNSHEND

THERE WAS amazement yesterday when a top name from the world of showbiz was sensationally discovered not to be a paedophile.

Who Next?

The celebrity in question is alleged not to have downloaded child pornography from the internet nor to have molested any under-age children.

Said a spokesman for the celebrity, "This is a terrible mistake. My client is horrified at the suggestion that he is not a pervert. His explanation is simply that he was conducting research into normal behaviour and accidentally accessed a web page not showing obscene images of minors. It was this curiosity that led to his association with the world of non-deviants.

"This could be the end of his career," he added and *(cont. p. 94)*

POLICE DON'T SWOOP ON BURGLAR

by Our Crime Staff SCOTT FREE

IN A dramatic raid yesterday, a huge force of uniformed and Special Branch officers did not swoop on a suspected burglary at someone's house.

Said Inspector Knacker, "All twelve of us stayed in the station and ignored the burglary.

"It is unfortunate, but we do not have the resources to go around investigating crimes that do not involve celebrities.

Stars In Our Cells

"It takes twelve officers not to respond to petty crimes like burglary, robbery and mugging and we just can't spare the men from their celebrity duties."

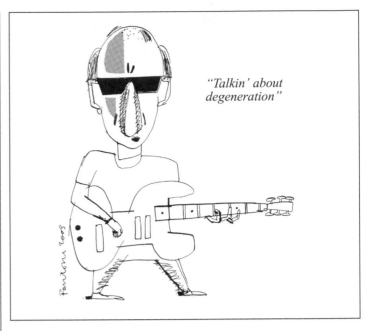

"Talkin' about degeneration"

MAN FOUND GUILTY BY JURY

by Our Crime Correspondent David Lynch Mob

THERE was outrage today after a man was found guilty of crime by a jury in a court.

"It's a disgrace," said one journalist, "and makes a mockery of this country's judicial system. It's long been a tradition in Britain that people are only found guilty once they have been tried by twelve good newspaper editors and true."

SHOCKING TRAGEDY INQUIRY FINDS TRAGEDY 'SHOCKING'

By Our Shocking Tragedy Correspondent Hans Wringing

THE INQUIRY into the shocking tragedy has concluded that something must be done. The conclusions will result in a dramatic overhaul of shocking tragedies, with the aim of ensuring that they never happen again.

The chairman of the enquiry, Lord Whyo'why, said of the shocking tragedy, "This must never happen again. Something must be done."

The inquiry recommended that:

● **This must never happen again.**

● **Something must be done.**

● **The government should appoint a Shocking Tragedy Commissioner, Ombudsman,** or Czar (though preferably all three).

● **The government should set up a new National Shocking Tragedy Agency.**

● **This must never happen again.**

The enquiry drew attention to the fact that there were too many agencies, and that communication between the agencies was poor. It is hoped that the creation of a brand new agency, the National Shocking Tragedy Agency, will help to rectify the problem of too many agencies. The role of the Shocking Tragedy Commissioner will be to facilitate improved communication between the Shocking Tragedy Ombudsman and the Shocking Tragedy Czar.

Counsellors coming to terms with not having been called to the disaster

37

HOUSE PRICE FALL MAY BRING FALL IN HOUSE PRICES – SHOCK NEWS

By Our Panic Staff
Clare Monger

BRITAIN was bracing itself today for a fall in house prices which would have a dramatic knock-on effect on property values.

"Make no mistake," said a leading expert, "the fall in house prices is going to mean that houses are worth less than they used to be. This in turn will mean that the property market will take a dive and that the bricks and mortar boom will be over."

He continued, "The government must act now. If house prices continue to fall, they won't go up any more.

"People may be worried about the war in Iraq and terrorist attacks at home but, compared to a fall in house prices, the end of the world seems pretty irrelevant."

POLLY FILLER

THAT'S IT! That's the last children's party I'm giving! Twenty demented five-year-olds screaming their heads off and throwing food around is not my idea of fun!

You would have thought that their mummies might try and control them, but think again – because of course the mothers *weren't there!* Instead an assortment of asylum seekers pretending to be nannies feebly attempted to stop their charges being rude to the entertainer – the hugely expensive and overrated Mr Twizzle, whose jokes were frankly inappropriate and whose balloon animals actually caused my son Charlie to burst into tears! Thanks a lot, Mr Swizzle! Charlie quite reasonably asked for a Tyrannosaurus Rex and was

fobbed off with a balloon giraffe. No wonder he set fire to Mr Twizzle's puppet theatre!

Needless to say, it's all the fault of the useless Simon, who should have booked HMS Belfast as planned, or even the Imperial War Museum or the London Dungeon sleepover, but oh no – he was too busy watching Extreme Celebrity Backgammon introduced by Victoria Coren on BBC Plus World 3 and then it was too late!

So poor Charlie and his mates had to make do with tea at Soho House and an apology for an entertainer whose act was completely thrown by something as minor as a medium-sized fire. Unprofessional or what?

And is it just me? Or are other people's children incredibly badly brought up? This lot had no manners and weren't even slightly sympathetic when the birthday boy threw up his chocolate gateau into their going-home bags. Honestly, I blame the parents for indulging their little brats and producing a generation of what I call greedy and self-obsessed mini-monsters.

I AM only grateful that I witnessed this fiasco on video rather than in person since as a working mum I was taking a well-earned and desperately needed battery-charging two-week break in the French Alps.

Had I been at the party I would at least have made a decent job of recording the event, as opposed to the ham-fisted attempt by the inept Lönka. A word of advice for next time, dear – on the Canon Elura MCV80 the zoom facility button is on the right. The one on the left activates the anti-shake hand control system! Honestly! Don't

they teach these Kosovan girls anything these days!

Next year I am going to organise Charlie's party myself – in fact I've already done so and booked Sabrina at "Surprise Surprise Party Organisers" (Notting Hill) to make sure there are no mistakes!

And one last word – whichever dim woman gave Charlie the Harry Potter 2 video game as a present – he's got it already, for heaven's sake, which makes your thoughtlessness a real waste of £44.99!!

Call yourself a mother!

©Polly Filler.

COMING SOON 200,000 AFFORDABLE HOMES

The BBC Iraq Debate

(Studio full of presenters and experts. Solemn music plays.)

Jeremy Vine: Now with Saddam refusing yet again to comply with the weapons inspectors, the big question on everyone's lips has to be 'Should I be wearing a tie?'

Military Expert: Well, the evidence is not conclusive and we cannot say for certain...

Jeremy Paxman: Come on – yes or no. Is this open-necked shirt-effect silly or not?

General: If I could come in there, I think the surveillance pictures show that...

Matt Frei: Surely it's good to look casual? You know – modern, 'with it', accessible, not too stuffy?

Admiral: The important issue is whether the

link between Saddam Hussein and the Al-Qaeda terrorist network has been...

Jeremy Vine: You're avoiding the question, aren't you? What about a polo neck?

Jeremy Paxman: Or a polo shirt?

Matt Frei: What about a t-shirt? Or a sweatshirt? Or no shirt at all? Is that too casual?

Foreign Secretary: I fail to see what...

Jeremy Vine: I'm sorry, that's all we've got time for. If you have a view on the new BBC policy of casual dress code, you can email us on dumbdown@bbc.co.uk or text us on 073742845 or alternatively you can just forget it because it doesn't really matter.

(More solemn music. Credits.)

Exclusive to Private Eye and all other newspapers

Leading celebrities explain their differing stances on Bush's War.

RICK PEEBLE (Dave Smith in ITV's Paravets)

I AM totally against the war because it's just about oil, isn't it? And I'm against that, as a way of life.

TRISH YOBB (DJ on Radio One's Yobb Show)

AS A woman, I am totally against Bush's genocidal policy. War is never right, unless of course there is a second UN resolution.

HARVEY TURNUP (Designer for The House of Turnup, Jermyn Street)

IF I was called up, I wouldn't go. People get killed in wars, you know. Everyone forgets that.

CINDY TOOTHBRUSH (Fashion model)

I HATE Blair. You can't believe a word he says. And the whole thing's ridiculous to my mind. I'm against.

RICKY CHEESE (Alternative comedian and star of BBC3's new topical youth show, 'Hard Cheese')

BUSH? Adolf Bush? Right? Makes me sick. Right? Think about it.

SAY 'NO' TO THE MIRROR

MILLIONS of people have joined the Eye's campaign and signed the anti-Mirror petition. Letters, faxes and text messages have been flooding into our offices demanding that Piers Moron stops trying to use the anti-war movement as an excuse to sell his paper.

Generals, diplomats, church leaders, TV celebrities and soap stars have all been harassed by the Mirror in their desperate attempts to stop losing the circulation war.

Now **you** can **stop** them.
Cut out and send this coupon now.

Mr Moron, I hereby register my opposition to the stance in your paper which is not justified by any evidence of previous interest in political journalism or moral and intellectual debate.

NAME..

ADDRESS...
....

NOT IN YOUR NAME

Bill Deedes
Writes

When I saw the photos of our fine, clean-shaven young servicemen kissing their sweethearts goodbye as they embarked for the Gulf, my thoughts inevitably went back to the similar scenes I witnessed at the outbreak of another war.

As a young reporter, I was moved by the sound of the bands playing, the flags flying, the girls in hats handing out white feathers to anyone not in uniform.

And there, striding manfully through the crowd to board the troopship, was the Duke of Wellington himself. *(Or was it Henry V? Please check.)*

Some things never change, this column being a prime example (and Nelson's Column another).

☐ EVERYONE I know is worried about the new plague of our time – magpies. What is to be done about them? Nobody knows. Wasn't it Lord Nelson who suggested that *(cont'd 1494)*.

Nature notes with "Old Ron"

This is the perfect time of year to get out into the woods in the hope of seeing buggers in their natural habitat. Mostly the bugger is a shy, nocturnal creature, who can be easily distinguished by his bushy moustache and his shiny leather jacket. But during the mating season, which is all year round, the buggers will come out in broad daylight, to romp about and play their little games. They will even let photographers near enough to take pictures of them, and ruin my career. As I said at the time, "Well, I'll be badgered!".

Ron Davies,
The Old Problem,
Clapham, London

"Yes, well, that's the problem living on such a busy road"

THOSE BAFTAS IN FULL

Sir Stephen Spry *(for it is he)*: And here to introduce the next award is the moist and multifellatius, the orgasmically overblessed maestro of the moustache, Sir Ian Goosy Gandalf...

Sir Ian McKellan *(for it is her)*: Ooh, er... cheeky monkey! *(Puts on serious face.)* My Lords, Ladies, Members of the Academy, it is my very great privilege to announce the nominations for Most Serious Film.

(Shot of dim actresses suddenly looking very serious in audience.)

Sir Gandalf: And the nominations are Stephen Dreary for "Two Suicides and a Funeral" *(Sombre applause.)*, Martin Scorphewwhatastinker for "The Hats of New York".

(More sombre applause. Shot of Daniel Day-Release with shaved head.)

Dame Serena McLuvvie: And Roman Polanski for his incredible autobiographical film "The Paedophile". *(Surely "The Pianist"? Ed.)*

(Even more sombre applause at mention of Holocaust but no mention of statutory rape charge involving under-age girl.)

And the winner is Roman Holiday.

(Audience stand to give ovation to some man representing fugitive pianist. [Surely 'paedophile'? Ed.])

Sir Crispin Fry: Well, the Great Dame of Time has wound her weary gusset around the Delphic orifice that is this event and we must move on to the next of our cornucopia of cunnilinguistical categories (and there's something to get your tongue around), it's the Lifetime of Making Money Award which tonight goes to the extraordinary Solly J. Brolly whose legendary career spans *(continues in similar vein for 94 hours)*

The Daily Kyliegraph

Britain's biggest-selling quality daily   Friday, February 7, 2003

Exclusive – Kylie shows us her knickers

by Editor **Charles Phwoar**

TODAY the Daily Telegraph is proud and privileged to present to its readers some really hot pix of Kylie's bum in some great stretch-knickers.

And there's more for you lingerie lovers!! Suspender belts, stockings, bras – the lot!

Corrrr!!

On Other Pages
Why Britain lacks any moral direction. First in a series of interviews by **Grayman Turner** with leading Catholic theologians.

© *The Kylie Telegraph*

TOMORROW
The Daily Tatugraph – Teen Lesbian Issue!

ANTHONY HOPKINS MARRIES

She's an antique collector

I've got a good one here

"Ha ha – I can't see your knickers! I can't see your knickers!"

Prudential Call Centre, Bombay

Schott's Original Telegraph Miscellany

A gallimaufry of vital irrelevance and uncommon knowledge compiled by **Phil Space** *(Surely 'Ben Schott'? Ed.)*

NOTABLE JOHNSONS
Boris
Boris's sister, Rachel
Boris's dad, Frank

MOST POPULAR ALMA MATER
Eton
Eton
Eton

CARTOONISTS WITH HONOURS
Nick Garland OBE
Matt OBE
Peattie and Taylor MBE

NAMES OF TOM KEMP'S CHILDREN
Tom
Clovis
Peregrine
Rumpelstiltskin

FAMOUS COLUMNISTS WITH 2 INITIALS
A.N. Wilson
W.F. Deedes
D.J. Taylor
The Late T.E. Utley

WRITERS' REAL AGES
Adam Nicholson 78 (24)
Sarah Sands 11 (93)
Alexander Chancellor 103 (74)
James Le Fanu 94 (94)
Bill Deedes 22 (197)

LONGEST BEARDS

Christopher Howse 34.3cms
Mark Steyn 2.2cms
Joshua Rozenbeard 94cms

MOST DIFFICULT CROSSWORD CLUE
"Boring Editor found when heir to the throne meets Othello with ecstasy" (7,5)
(That's enough Schott's Miscellany)

IN THE COURTS

Mr George Michael Douglas Fairbanks Jr and Her Royal Highness Princess Catherine Armstrong-Jones of Zeta v. *Hullo!* Magazine

Before Mr Justice Cocklecarrot

Day 94

Cocklecarrot: Your Highness, may I say what an honour it is that you should grace our humble courtroom with your writ. Not since last week, when we were privileged to have a video link with St John of Cleese, have I had such a famous person in the back of my court!

(Sycophantic laughter from 2000 assembled hacks.)

Would you like to sit down, Miss Jones, since you are not only very famous and beautiful, but also pregnant and the innocent victim of one of the gravest *scandala magnata* that has ever been perpetrated by the so-called gentlemen of the press.

Miss Zeta-Jones: You are too kind, your Worshipfulness.

(Takes seat offered by usher.)

Cocklecarrot: Mr Hugefee, pray explain to the court the circumstances of this dreadful case.

Sir Ephraim Hugefee QC *(for Miss Zebra-Crossing)*: Will you please tell the court what were your feelings when you first saw the photographs of your wedding in this shameless, disgusting and opprobrious publication viz. the *Hullo!* magazine.

Miss Zeta-Minus *(taking out Welsh onion [possibly leek])*: Sob. No words can describe my feelings of shock, horror, hurt, insult, umbrage, humiliation and outrage when I saw pictures of myself in my wedding dress in the magazine in question. What should have been the happiest day of my life had been cruelly violated and turned into a living nightmare which will haunt me to my dying day.

(Hacks break into spontaneous applause, judge weeps openly.)

Was that alright, Michael? Or do you think I should have held back a bit at the beginning and then really milked it at the end. Shall I take it from the top?

Mr Michael Douglas *(for it is he)*: Darling, you were wonderful. Waddya say, judge, does the lady get an Oscar, or does she get an Oscar?

Mr Justice Cocklecarrot: Pray sit down, Mr Dougal, you are not in Spartacus now. Proceed Miss Jones, and if you would care to remove any excess clothing, please feel free to do so. It is getting rather hot in here. Perhaps the usher could turn the heating up.

(The court then heard that Mr and Mrs Douglas were entitled to claim unprecedented damages for the invasion of their privacy

ZETA-JONES PICTURE ROW

perpetrated by the photographers of Hullo! *magazine, who should have left them alone to be photographed exclusively on behalf of the* OK *magazine and its much-respected proprietor Lord Desmond of Filth. Miss Zed-List was then cross-examined by Sir Grately Overprice QC on behalf of Lord Asian of Babes.)*

Overprice: Miss Beta-Max, would you care to look at these charming photographs of yourself eating a delicious piece of cake. I submit that nothing could be more delightful than this scene.

Miss Indiana Jones: Now you listen here, boyo. I've had about enough of you, you posh git. One more slimy remark like that and you get it in the mouth.

Cocklecarrot: Miss Zed-Cars, although everyone in this courtroom will be deeply sympathetic to your feelings of outrage in being forced to answer questions instead of being simply handed a cheque for £1 million, I'm afraid that you must do your best to assist the court.

Miss Tom-Jones: I'm sorry, Your Worship, my feelings ran away with me.

Kirk Douglas: Don't overdo it, sweetie, they're eating out of your hand. Don't blow it now.

Cocklecarrot: I notice that it is already half-past eleven and time for luncheon. If you are free, Miss Peter-Jones, I should be delighted to escort you to the Ladies Annexe at the Garrick, where they serve a delicious plate of fish. You, Mr Dougal, will, I am sure, welcome the opportunity to stay here, to prepare yourself for this afternoon's performance. Perhaps you could look over your lines.

Usher: Pray be upstanding for Miss Zeta-Jones.

(The case continues.)

ST CAKES TO REMAIN 'ALL RICH'

by **St Hilda Thatcher**

THE prestigious £24,000-a-term Midlands independent boarding school St Cakes (motto 'quis paget entrant' – 'who pays gets in') has decided to remain a bastion against the egalitarianism of the modern world by refusing to allow poor parents to send their children there.

The vote to keep St Cakes "all rich" was a unanimous one, taken by the headmaster Mr R.J. Kipling.

"We wanted to preserve a traditional 'rich' atmosphere," he explained, "where our pupils do not have to face all the distractions associated with the presence of poor people.

"Our exam results," he went on, "show the undoubted advantage of single-income-band education. We got our last GCSE in 1987 and we don't want our record ruined."

From the cabdrivers of London

An Apology To Mr Ken Livingstone Over The Introduction Of The Congestion Charge February 2003

That Red Ken, you've got to hand it to him. Bloody brilliant. I know last week we all said he should be strung up because it was the only language he understood. But to a man us cabbies are putting our hands up and saying, "Ken, you're a diamond mayor. You was right and we was wrong." Credit where it's due. Take this morning, right! I am at Euston and pick up this fare who wants to go to the Aldwych. Normally, in rush-hour traffic, you're looking at an hour and a half. But this morning it took me eleven minutes. I checked it on my watch. I mean, I've driven a cab on Christmas Day and there's been more traffic than there is with this congestion charge. No, he's a very clever man. Very clever indeed. I had that Steven Norris in the back of the cab once. Now there's someone who should be strung up. What a prat.

Issued on behalf of the Operators of Taximeter Carriages and Licensed Cabriolets in the Greater London Area. February 2003.

● *If you've recently been in a taxi or you have strong views about the congestion charge, send us your comments at www.stringemup.gov*

WIDOW OPENS JOHN LENNON HOUSE

by Our Heritage Staff **Lunchtime O'No**

YOKO ONO yesterday donated John Lennon's childhood home to the people of Britain.

In a moving ceremony attended by thousands of journalists, the widow of the greatest Briton who ever lived, showed the press around the two-bedroom semi in Liverpool where history was made.

"This is where I taught John how to play the guitar," said the famous Oriental performance artist, pointing to the bathroom where the young Lennon dreamed up his early hits.

Can't Imagine The Point

"And this," she continued, as she moved into a small single bedroom, "is where I gave birth to John all those years ago, after I had received a message from the Archangel Gabriel."

How to get there

Virgin train to McCartney International Station, the 147 Bus to Harrison Roundabout, then taxi to Ringo Starr Memorial Shopping Mall, then ask someone the way.

● Open Monday-Friday 9-5, weekends 2-6, Entrance Free, OAPs £10.

National Trust Rating: Z-z-z-z-z

THE treatment of Matthew Kelly has been little short of a national scandal. One of our best-loved TV performers has been made to endure a living hell of baseless innuendo and unfounded suspicion which threatened to end his entire career. All this *ON NO EVIDENCE AT ALL.*

Brave Matthew was targeted solely because of his celebrity in a smear campaign of hate and lies.

Today he stands a totally innocent man. But there *are* guilty men in this shocking story. Ourselves. *(Surely the police? Ed.)*

ON OTHER PAGES

● 100s of pix of Kelly looking a bit weird **2**
● Can there be no smoke without fire? **3**
● Unfunny 'Stars in your underpants'cartoon by repentant Mac **94**

To The Editor Of The Guardian

We, the undersigned, all members of the British Rabbit Breeders Association, wish to put on record our unqualified opposition to any war in Iraq, unless sanctioned by a second UN resolution.

**Frank Angora
R.B.J. Shuttleworth
Rachel Smelt
The Bishop of Oxford
Suleiman Papadoulis
Angela Ziegler**

**Nathan Ferret
Lady Natasha Rufus-Isaacs
and 214 others**

(You can see the full list on our website: *www.rabbitbreedersagainstthewar.com*)

● I hope the American 'smart bombs' are a good deal smarter than the American President.

Mike Giggler
(Via e-mail)

DAME THORA HIRD R.I.P.

Those SHERIDAN MORLEY MEMOIRS In Full

Chapter One

Z -z-z-z-z-z-z-z-z-z-z-z-z-z-z-z-z-z-z-z-z-z-z-z-z-z-z-z-z-

Lookalikes

Berlusconi　　　　**Shrek**

Sir,
　　Are they related?
　　　　Yours,
　　　　SCOTT THOMSON,
Edinburgh.

Hancock　　　　**Brown**

Sir,
　　Re: Lookalike in Letters 1074. I have noticed an unsettling similarity between the Rt. Hon. Gordon Brown MP and the late Anthony Aloysius St John Hancock of 23 Railway Cuttings, East Cheam.
　　Stone me, could they be related?
　　　　Yours faithfully,
　　　　N.F. COOK,
Nottingham.

Dobby　　　　**Charles**

Sir,
　　I was struck by the resemblance of our glorious King-to-be with the equally wonderful fantasy figure of Dobby from Harry Potter. Certainly they both share a masochistic tendency to beat themselves about the head with alarming consistency.
　　　　Yours faithfully,
　　　　JOHN BROOKS,
London SE23.

Sir,
　　I am worried by the uncanny resemblance between US Secretary of State Colin Powell and Mictlantecuhtli, Aztec god of death. Are the Iraqis in even deeper trouble than they thought?
　　　　Yours faithfully,
　　　　ROBERT SOLOMON,
London NW3.

Powell　　　　**Aztec god**

Dim　　　　**Hewitt**

Sir,
　　I have noticed an uncanny resemblance between James Hewitt, as he recently appeared on the Larry King show, and Harry Enfield's "Tim Nice But Dim" character.
　　Are they by any chance related?
　　　　E. HARMAN,
High Wycombe, Bucks.

Ken　　　　**"Goon"**

Sir,
　　I have noticed an uncanny resemblance between Ken Livingstone, mayor of London, and one of the mayor of South Park's "goons". Are they by any chance related?
　　　　K. CONNELL,
Camberley, Surrey.

Posh　　　　**Jackson**

Sir,
　　I have noticed an uncanny resemblance between Michael Jackson and Victoria Beckham. I wonder if by any chance they are related?
　　　　Yours faithfully,
　　　　ED HARMAN,
High Wycombe

Saddam Hussein　　　　**Mr Potato Head**

Sir,
　　Is there something we're not being told?
　　　　TOBY FEDER (aged 3),
Via email.

McCartney　　　　**Milburn**

Sir,
　　Separated at birth? Will Mr Alan Milburn have the same gift of the gab gene as Sir Paul to convince people that NHS Foundations Trusts are for public benefit?
　　　　Yours faithfully,
　　　　ELIZABETH MILLS,
Newcastle-under-Lyme, Staffs.

Abu Hamza　　　　**Richard Wilson**

Sir,
　　Lookalike or just look out for pirates?
　　　　All best,
　　　　PETER CUNDALL,
London NW1.

Eminem　　　　**Mother Teresa**

Sir,
　　Has anybody noticed the resemblance between the soon to be sainted Mother Teresa of Calcutta and bad boy of rap Eminem?
　　Both are/were considered to be voices for the underprivileged but until now only one of them has been credited with performing miracles.
　　I suspect they are related and think we should be told.
　　　　ENA B. MAXWELL,
Uganda House, Neasden.

Galloway **Loyalist**

Sir,

This photograph of a commander of the Republican Guard reminds me strangely of George Galloway.

But I am sure that they cannot possibly be related.

ENA B. TUDOR,

Via email.

Susan **Laurence**

Sir,

I wonder if fear of tonsorial abuse is the only thing that American feminist Susan Sontag shares with TV's Laurence Llewelyn-Bowen? Surely not chintz?

Yours,
ENA B. RUSHTON,

London SW6.

Mugabe **Tamarind Seed**

Sir,

The uplifting picture of Our Lord revealed in a peanut, published in your last edition, bought to mind that 1974 "lost classic" of the cinema, The Tamarind Seed, starring Omar Sharif and Julie Andrews. The eponymous seed was supposed to bear the likeness of an unfortunate black man who, so the legend goes, was hanged from the branches of its progenitor. Imagine my surprise, therefore, when munching upon a Tamarind the other day, to discover the enclosed. By any chance, could this miraculous fruit have been foretelling the imminent demise of any well-known statesman? I think he should be told.

Yours faithfully,
STEVEN HAINES,

Via e-mail.

John **John**

Sir,

Has anyone noticed the remarkable similarity between Sir Elton John, the very openly gay rock musician and Dr Jeffrey John, one of the Church of England's leading homosexual rights advocates?

Are they in any way related?

RICHARD LEESON,

Via email.

Prince **Beavis**

Sir,

Look. There is a clear resemblance between His Royal Highness Prince Harry and Beavis (cohort of Butthead). Is it too much to hope that they might be related?

God Save The Queen!
JIM RUSSELL,

Cambridge.

Lawson **Keeler**

Sir,

One the friend of a Cabinet Minister and the other the daughter of a Cabinet Minister; one a Domestic Goddess and one a Sex Goddess. Is there any chance that Christine Keeler and Nigella Lawson could actually be the same person?

Yours,
ANN HALL,

Erith, Kent.

Al-Assad **Darling**

Sir,

I'd just like to say how disappointed I was to hear former World War I patriot Captain Darling criticise the Allied operation to free the Iraqis now that he's become president of Syria. Didn't Melchett teach him anything? I think we should be told.

Yours faithfully,
S. TOWNSEND,

London.

Hussein **Davies**

Sir,

I recently spotted this lookalike of Saddam Hussein, a man who knows a thing or two about lookalikes.

Yours sincerely,
RICK YATES,

Via email.

Caveman **Holder**

Sir,

I could not help noticing a resemblance between Noddy Holder (ex-Slade) and the caveman on the front of a recent TV listing.

I wonder if they are related – as indeed we all are.

RICHARD BEASLEY,

Winchester, Hants.

Brand **Sergeant**

Sir,

"Have I Got News For You?" has finally solved the mystery. John Sergeant seems to bear an uncanny resemblance to Jo Brand without the wig. Or... Jo Brand bears an uncanny resemblance to John Sergeant WITH a wig! Are they in any way related?

PETER ARNOLD

Canterbury, Kent.

Sir,

Has anyone noticed the resemblance between collagen-enhanced tv starlet Leslie Ash, Fizz from the Tweenies and Lisa Weever from the Comfort fabric conditioner ads? Are they by any chance related? I think we should be told.

Sincerely,
JOHN WILLIAMS,

Via email.

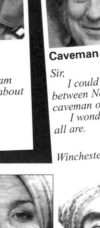

Fizz **Leslie** **Lisa**

That Smoking Tape In Full

The Final Proof That Saddam Is In League With Al Qaeda

Osama bin Laden (*for it is possibly he*): That Saddam – what a bastard. Doesn't believe in Islam? Bloody infidel! Do you know what I'd do to him? String 'im up! It's the only language he understands. Socialist scum.

I had that George Bush in the back of my cave once. But I got away. A very stupid man.

© Al Cabeera, the TV station that taxi drivers trust.

AL QAEDA SUSPECT ARRESTED

by Our Security Staff **Lunchtime O'Nowevegotthewrongman**

POSSIBLY the world's most wanted terrorist was today seized as he was having dinner with Prince Charles.

The bearded fanatic is thought to have been one of Osama bin Laden's top henchmen in the fight against America and has long been on the FBI's list of "Most Bearded Men".

Said a senior FBI source, "we were tipped off about this fanatical bearded cleric whom we think is the world's most dangerous man".

Later, it emerged that the FBI had made a mistake, and that the so-called terrorist was an innocent Archbishop of Canterbury.

Said the FBI source, "It was an unfortunate case of mistaken

identity. Rowan Williams is the wrong man. We meant to arrest Mr David Blunkett."

Said the Archbishop, "I think it was St Anselm who said that if we search deep into *(cont. p. 94)*

*"I don't **think** they are soldier ants"*

BUSH ATTACKS CRITICS

SADDAM ATTACKS BUSH

EVERYONE ATTACKS COUGH

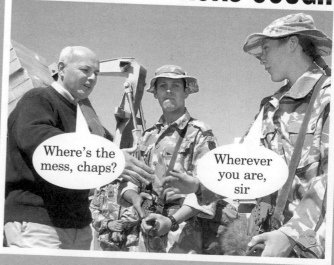

DAILY TELEGRAPH

The Scumbag Who Won't Back Our Boys

BY OUR POLITICAL STAFF
BORIS NOTGODUNOV

AS THOUSANDS of British troops prepare to risk their lives in the scorching desert sun of Iraq, Liberal Democrat leader Charles "Chamberlain" Kennedy last night raised the white flag in a craven bid to appease the most evil dictator in the history of the world.

The quisling Kennedy, following in the limp-wristed tradition of Jeremy Thorpe and Lord Haw-Haw, stated categorically that he would not support the British troops who are preparing to risk their lives in *(You've done this bit. Ed.)*

Coward

Said Mrs Caroline Madeup-Name (whose son Lieut. Simon Madeup-Name sailed for the Gulf only yesterday), "Charles Kennedy makes me ashamed to be British – to think of our boys dying in the sand while he sits swilling whisky in the House of Commons makes you sick.

"I will never vote Lib Dem again," she told the Telegraph last night. "From now on it will be Tory every time."

On Other Pages

Christopher Howse on "Is Roman Catholicism the new Conrad Black?"

Exclusive interview with Britain's leading Catholic laywoman – St Cheresa of Booth QC.

Yes, it's all in the super soaraway Daily Tabletgraph!

Radio Highlights

The Today Programme

Jim Naughtie *(for it is he)*:And now Iraq. We have in the studio President George Bush and Saddam Hussein. If I can turn to you first, President Bush, what you're saying basically is – and correct me if I'm wrong – look, Saddam has had twelve years to disarm and this has nothing to do with oil or unfinished business left by your father when he was in the White House...

Bush: I would just like to...

Naughtie: ...because that's the nub of your position, isn't it? You believe that Saddam represents a real threat to world peace, even though there's no evidence of any definite connection with Al Qaeda, and even though the weapons of mass destruction that you've said so much about, haven't been found yet...

Hussein: May I just say...

Naughtie: ...of course, your view is diametrically opposed to that of Mr Bush here. As I understand it, you feel that it is the United States which is engaged in an imperialist adventure, without the support of the international community as expressed through the United Nations.

Bush: Excuse me, Mr Naughtie, could I correct...

Naughtie: ...no, you'll be able to put your side of the case in a minute, but I think we have to let Mr Hussein make his point which, as I see it, is that Resolution 1441 does not in itself authorise...

Hussein: Please, Mr Naughtie, you must allow me...

Naughtie: Look, if everyone talks at once, our listeners won't be able to hear the question.

Bush and Hussein *(together)*:

What is the question?

Naughtie: Gentlemen, thank you. I'm sorry, that's all we've got time for. And now, Thought For The Day, with His Holiness Shri Hari Enfield, chief guru of the Hari Krishna Temple in Enfield.

Enfield: You know, when I read about the Congestion Charge, I thought "Aren't all our lives suffering from congestion these days?" I know minc is... *(Cont'd. 94 Khz)*

YES! IT'S BROWN NOSE DAY

All your favourite TV stars will be making themselves look even more ridiculous than usual, and it's all for a good cause – world war.

Join funsters Tony Blair, Pete Mandelson, Jackie Straw, Iain Duncan Laugh and a whole host of larger-than-life comedians as they attempt to do silly stunts to raze Baghdad to the ground.

This year's Brown Nose Day promises to be the most spectacular ever, as these comical celebs line up to "brown nose" George Bush!

MISGUIDED MISSILE

"Of course it's great the public are behind us on this one"

47

MOMENT OF TRUTH... DESTINY CALLS... WORLD ON THE BRINK... TIME FOR CLICHE... ETC

by Our Entire Staff **Phil Pages**

YES, there is no doubt about it – today marks the moment of truth when destiny calls with the world on the brink.

History will record that it was on this day that the clichés were finally unleashed and *(cont. p. 94)*

Why It Is Legal To Go To War

by Our Legal Staff **Marcel Berlinwall**

THE ATTORNEY General, Lord Goldsmith, has reassured the Prime Minister that any war against Iraq is not only just but legal under an ancient British law called *De Bello Saddamico Conveniensis*, which dates all the way back to yesterday morning.

According to the ancient statute, "The First Minister of the British Nation, whomsoever he may be, shall have the inalienable right to declare war on behalf of His Majesty's government without let or hindrance from any foreign bodies whomsoever they may be

or any of his ministers who may calleth him reckless or the unruly populace of the country or any French person who may attempt to invoke divers bogus laws (*Lex Bogi*) which shall be deemed 'an unreasonable veto'. All of which quite obviously alloweth the Prime Minister to do whatever he so desireth with the full might and majesty of the law of the United States of America."

Signed
The Lord High Chancellor
Lord Lairg
The Year of Our Lord 1122

On Other Pages ■ Is the document a forgery?

Exclusive To All Papers

OUR BOYS READY TO GO IN

by Our War Staff **Phil Acres**

AS THE countdown to war reaches its final conclusion, the dedicated men and women of the graphics department are on red alert – ready to drop into the newspaper at a moment's notice.

Armed with the latest technology (Apple Macs) they can deliver an amazing range of graphics with very little warning. "We are talking coloured maps, cutaway drawings of tanks, floor plans of Saddam's bunker, little men representing the Republican Guard and big black arrows everywhere," said one veteran.

"This is what we've been training for and we're very keen to get on with the job. We are

How It Will Look – The Sort Of Black Arrows You Will See

confident that we'll cover a huge amount of space on the first day and it will only be a week or so before we can go back to illustrating articles asking whether the Pyramids were early space stations."

THE WEEK IN PICTURES

BRITISH DIPLOMACY

AMERICAN DIPLOMACY

INTERNATIONAL DIPLOMACY

48

NORTH KOREA'S DEAR LEADER WON GREAT APPROVAL FOR HIS NEW COIFFURE FROM AN ADMIRING MILITARY COUNCIL

Lynda Lee-Potter

Why this vain, self-righteous woman should keep her moral lectures to herself

DOESN'T it make you sick, the sight of this arrogant, sanctimonious hypocrite parading her conscience all over the media and pretending she's only doing it for the public good?

But enough of me. That Clare Short *(contd. p.94)*

49

PARLIAMENTARY DEBATES

Select Committee On The Very Important Issue Of Self-Regulation By The Press

Mr Gerald Kaufperson (Chairman): Mr Moron, you are the editor, are you not, of the Daily Mirror. Can you please tell the Committee...

Mr Piers Moron *(for it is he):* Don't you threaten me, you bald bastard. I know where you live and a lot more besides...

Kaufperson: Mr Moron, I must ask you to remember that you are appearing before this very important committee of very important MPs, of which I am the most important.

Moron: Shut up you four-eyed git and stop poncing around. The British tabloid press, of which the Daily Mirror is the finest example, has never served the British public, not to mention the entire human race, better than it is doing now...

Kaufperson: It ill behoves you, Mr Moron, to make these uncouth interruptions. I must warn you that you are not in your office at the Daily Moron now, and that...

Moron: ...the tabloids today are wholly responsible, non-intrusive, sensitive and dedicated to nothing but the highest standards of decency, truth and probity, and if you don't put that in your effing report I will make up some filth about your private life and run it on the front page.

Kaufperson: I am indebted to you, Mr Moron. No further questions. Call the next witness, Miss Rebekah Wade. Miss Wade, you are, are you not, the Editor of the Sun newspaper?

Miss Wadinginfilth *(for it is she)*: Nah, that is Mr Rupert Murdoch. I'm just paid to put in what he tells me. A very clever man.

Kaufperson: I put it to you, Miss Wade, that you have paid money to the police for confidential information?

Wade: 'course I have, everyone does it. *(Mobile goes off noisily as Ms Wade studies txt msg from 'drty dggr'.)* I now realise that the Sun newspaper has never paid members of the police service for information as this would be contrary to our Code of Ethics.

Kaufperson: There seems to be some element of ambiguity in your answer to the Committee, Miss Wade.

Wade: Shutupyaface, baldilocks! I'm sure we can pay some copper to name and shame you as one of them...

Kaufperson: I am indebted to you, Miss Wade. I think we can leave it there *(contd column 94)*

RGJ

THAT ROYAL HERNIA OPERATION TIMETABLE IN FULL

Monday	Prince Charles is operated on and surgeons will remove the swelling.
Monday night	The swelling will be passed on to Michael Fawcett.
Tuesday	The swelling will disappear out of the back door of St James's Palace into an unmarked white van.
Friday	The swelling will be on sale at a local antiques shop.

That's the closest you're going to get, mate

SEARCH FOR TERROR LEADER CONTINUES

FOLLOWING reports that Osama Bin Laden had shaved off his beard in an attempt to evade capture, the Government has released this photo-fit of the world's most evil person for identification purposes and has warned the country to be on the look-out.

HOW HE LOOKED   **HOW HE MIGHT LOOK NOW**

"You earn good money at the circus, why can't we buy mother a proper stairlift"

Man With Tie: ...and now, to remind viewers who may just have joined us, the main news is that the key town of Bagpuz has been secured by coalition forces. We're now going over live to our reporter in the front line just outside Bagpuz, Andy McPandy. Andy, can you tell us what's the latest on the situation there?

(We see man in combat gear, only partially visible due to sandstorm.)

McPandy *(for it is he)*: Well, Trevor, the situation in Bagpuz is very confused. But our information is that, at this moment in time, coalition forces have secured this key town. I spoke earlier to a senior coalition commander, Brigadier Whittam-Smith.

(Film clip of Brigadier also in sandstorm.)

McPandy: Can you confirm for me that Bagpuz has been secured by coalition forces?

Brigadier Whittam-Smith: Well, I've just been watching CNN and they tell me that Bagpuz has definitely been secured. I'm afraid I can't say more than that at this stage.

McPandy: So there we are, Roger, confirmation of probably the most significant event in the war so far: that this key town has fallen to coalition forces.

(In background we see Iraqi flag being raised over Bagpuz. Caption runs along bottom of screen: 'Bagpuz secure – it's official'. We then cut back to studio.)

Blonde Woman *(sitting next to man in tie)*: General Cordite, you led the 51st Armoured Fusiliers in the first Gulf War. Would you say the fall of Bagpuz is the turning point in the war so far?

Brig. Cordite: Well, Bagpuz is on the strategically vital road connecting Bagheera to Sherekhan. So it was a town which the coalition forces simply had to make secure if they were to guarantee the supply line between the American 78th Infantry Division on the Euphrates and the 101st Armoured Brigade on the Tigris.

(Huge map appears on screen showing location of Bagpuz, with red graphic of small tank exploding next to it.)

Blonde Woman: Professor

Nerdsworth, you are the reader in strategic studies at the University of Solihull – can I come to you here? This is a pretty major victory at Bagpuz, isn't it? Would you say that it is the turning point of the entire war so far?

Prof. Nerdsworth: Yes, well, what you've got to remember is that this is the first fully televised war, where we know exactly what's happening and can see it on our screens as it happens.

(We see film clip labelled 'Breaking Story', showing cheering Iraqi troops carrying pictures of Saddam Hussein as they parade through the main square of Bagpuz.)

Man In Tie: Well, it seems the situation in Bagpuz is rather more confused than it appeared a few minutes ago. But we've now got to go over live to the capital Baghdad where our reporter Goldie Locks is witnessing the latest coalition air raid. Goldie, tell us what you can see from your hotel room.

(Cut to woman watching Abu Dhabi TV in hotel room.)

Goldie Locks: Well, Philip, the sky of Baghdad is once again being lit up by a series of massive explosions. You can hear them from the television that I'm watching. It's a truly awesome sight, this Abu Dhabi TV.

(Caption below screen: 'Bagpuz Under Iraqi Control'.)

Man In Tie: So, Goldie, what's the feeling there in Baghdad among the ordinary Iraqis?

Goldie: Well, I think you have to remember, Simon, that this is the first fully televised war. And the ordinary Iraqis, sitting in their homes, are watching the same pictures from Abu Dhabi as we are. So that is bound to have an affect on their morale.

(Caption: 'Saddam Hussein Dead'.)

Man In Tie: And I'll have to interrupt you there, Goldie, because we're just getting a report, as yet unconfirmed, that Saddam Hussein is dead, possibly killed, in a "friendly fire" incident by members of his own armed forces. We're going over live to Washington, where our correspondent Jim Soundbite is outside the White House, with the latest on this sensational development.

Soundbite: Yes, well that's quite right, John. We've just heard from Donald Rumsfeld that the key town of Bagpuz has definitely been secured by coalition forces, and I have to say, as I was watching him on television, that it was a much more upbeat performance from Mr Rumsfeld than we have had for some time.

Man In Tie: Thank you, Jim. We'll have to leave it there because there's more very important news breaking from the key northern

border town of Doh, where our Global Affairs Editor-in-Chief Homer Simpson has got the latest on the rapidly changing situation there.

(Caption: 'Saddam Hussein Appears Live On TV. George Bush "Killed By Friendly Fire".' Fat man in overcoat seen looking extremely unhappy in front of green night sky where nothing is happening.)

Little Green Simbo *(for it is he)*: Well, Andrew, I'm standing here a few miles from the key border post of Doh, where the Kurdish enclave is threatened by Saddam's elite 413th Ba'athplug Irregulars. We can't actually see the Iraqis from here or, for that matter, the Kurdish Peshwarinaans, or indeed anything at all. But earlier this evening I was watching Abu Dhabi Television, and it was clear from where I am standing that the key town of Bagpuz had been secured by coalition forces which, of course, is news which will have enormous impact on the situation up here, miles from nowhere, where I've been sent because I'm so famous...

Blonde Woman: Well, that was Homer Simpson in Doh, up there on the northern border. General, can I bring you in here again? We've just seen that startling report from Homer Simpson in Doh. How do you think this fits into the overall picture we're getting of how the war is going on Day 94?

(Caption: 'Bush "Alive", Says Pentagon'.)

General Corduroy: Yes, well, I think we've now got a very clear picture of everything that's going on both to the north and to the south of Baghdad. And, of course, both of these areas will be very important as the next crucial phase of the war develops. What we don't yet know is what is happening to the west of Baghdad, and the big question there must be, "Why hasn't Abu Dhabi TV shown us any pictures of what is going on?".

(We see the same three film clips of planes taking off, guns firing in desert, explosions in sky on a continuous loop. Caption: 'Go to bed and stop watching this rubbish'.)

'SOLDIERS DIE IN WAR' SHOCK

by Our Military Staff **Philippa Front-Page**

THE WORLD was horrified yesterday when it was reported that several soldiers had been killed in the war in Iraq.

"We had no idea that war was like this," said a spokesman. "It has certainly opened our eyes to the fact that war is incredibly dangerous.

"Fortunately," he went on, "a lot more of their side seem to have died than ours, but it's still a bit of a shock." *(Reuters)*

Get down! It's the Americans!

ANOTHER 3,000 OF OUR BOYS GO IN

by Our Media Staff **Phil Middle-East**

THE HARD-PRESSED army of journalists covering the war in Iraq is to be bolstered by a reserve detachment of fresh reporters, it was announced last night.

This will come as good news to the thousands of battle-weary hacks who have been talking round the clock for the last 372 hours.

The fresh forces will relieve some of the most overstretched correspondents and take on the arduous duties of non-stop report filing from key areas in Iraq.

The move follows criticism that too few journalists had originally been sent to capture the war and that at a strength of only 300,000 the media would not be capable of winning the ratings war.

The Desert Hacks

Now, with the extra battalions of eager recruits, it can only be a matter of time before they outnumber the troops. *(Surely some mistake? Ed.)*

As a huge number of columns march towards the front pages *(cont'd p. 94)*

GLENDA SLAGG

FLEET STREET'S FRIENDLY FIRE!!?!?

■ TIN HATS off to our heroes who are risking their lives for our freedom!!! And shame on the weasel-worded beardie-weardie peacenik Robin Cook who says we should run up the white flag and invite Saddam into our homes to murder our children!!!?! Once again, brave Tommy Atkins has shown the world what it means to be a man – did you get that, Robin, you red-headed gutless little twerp!!?! No offence, Mr Cook, but do us a favour – stop shooting your mouth off and try shooting yourself instead!?!?

■ THREE CHEERS for Robin Cook! The only man who had the guts to say what we're all thinking – ie, stop this madness now and bring our brave boys home before any more of them die pointlessly in the desert sand!!!! Wake up, Britain, and listen to courageous Captain Cook – the new voice of the new Ballsy Britain??!?!

■ *RAGEH OMAAR – Don'tchaluv-him?!?!? He's the hunky hack in Baghdad who's got the nation's gals a-swoonin' and a-moonin' as they see his girlie good looks every night on the telly! For Gawd's sake, Greg Dyke, give him his own show and keep us lusty lasses lickin' our lips in the long dark days ahead!!?!? Mmmmm!!!!?!*

■ SEE THE OSCARS???! Blimey??!? That Catherine Zeta-Jones – fat or what???! Is it twins!?!?? Come off it, dear!???! There's at least a dozen in there!?!?

■ SPARE a thought for poor old Prince Charles and his Right Royal Hernia. How did he get it???! Perhaps Camilla could tell us??!?! They say it comes from excess physical activity – and I don't mean unveiling plaques and talking to plants!!! (Geddit??!?!)

HERE they are, Glenda's Baghdad Beefcakes:

● **Donald Rumsfeld** – OK, he may be mad, but he can invade my territory any day.!!! Geddit!?! Mmm!!! Shock 'n' awe!!!!

● **General Tommy Franks** – See above!?!?!

● **Dominique de Villepin** – Some people may be against the French, but I like them against me!????! Geddit!!?!?! I won't say "Non" when the tousle-haired Talleyrand comes around to my place brandishing his veto??!?!? (Geddit??!?!)

Byeeee!!!

"I knew him when he was just in Mine Disposal"

Troops Welcomed By Grateful Iraqis

BY OUR MAN IN CANARY WHARF CONRAD BLACKPROPAGANDA

ADVANCING coalition troops were given a warm welcome yesterday in every part of southern Iraq.

The soldiers were quickly surrounded by throngs of Iraqis, eager to greet them in the traditional local style with happy shouts of "Go home Yankee imperialist swine!"

They showered the advancing allied troops with gifts of grenades and bullets as a thank-you for their liberation from the hated tyranny of their beloved leader Saddam Hussein.

A Taxi Driver Writes

Each week a well-known cabbie is invited to comment on an issue of topical importance.

THIS WEEK: **Johnny Keegan** (Cab No. 1914-18) on the conduct of the war in Iraq.

If you ask me, guv, we're going about it in totally the wrong way. We've gone soft, pussyfooting around handing out chocolates to kids and worrying about killing a few civilians. Blimey, guv, it's a war, innit? I mean, the sooner it's over the better. So let's get on with it. It's time we went in hard and flattened the whole of Baghdad. And if people get killed, so be it. It's the only language they understand, them Iraqis. I had that Max Hastings in the back of my cab once. Very clever man. He'd soon sort 'em out.

NEXT WEEK: MIKE GOVE (Cab. No. 1945) on "Going For The Nuclear Option".

 ## That American Anti-French Menu In Full

Freedom Fries

– ✳ –

Selection of Freedom Cheeses

– ✳ –

Freedom Bread

– ✳ –

Salad with Freedom Dressing

PLUS

One Freedom Letter for use in Post-Meal Intercourse

Precision technology proves itself on battlefield

by Our Defence Staff **Pat Riot-Missil**

THE extraordinary advance in 21st-century computer-guided laser weapons technology has been demonstrated to devastating effect in the first week of the war.

The ability of American missile systems to lock on to British targets including warplanes, tanks and television crews has stunned observers.

Said one US ordnance expert: "With the progress we are making we should have neutralised the British forces by next week and will have secured London *(cont'd p. 94)*

(cont'd p. 94)

What You Didn't Hear
Radio Bore's Today Programme

J. Humphrys *(for it is he)*: ...and now we were hoping to speak down the line to Brigadier Update in Qatar. Can you hear me, Brigadier?

Update: Hullo, hullo, can anyone hear me?

Humbug: We seem to have lost the Brigadier there, so we'll just have to move on to the Defence Secretary, Geoff Hoon. Mr Hoon, you've just heard the fiasco with Brigadier Update, where he couldn't even get a proper phone to talk to us. Isn't this just typical of the way this war is being mismanaged on all fronts?

Hoon: Good morning, John.

Humbug: It's hopeless, isn't it, Mr Hoon? Nothing works. First you were telling us the war would be over in ten minutes. Now it's obvious that it's going to last forever and that Saddam is beating us hands down.

Hoon: Well, really I think that's a bit...

Humbug: No, could you kindly answer the question?

Brigadier: Hullo, is anybody there?

Humbug: I'm sorry, we've run out of time. And now, 'Thought For The Day', with Jonathan Mullah.

Mullah: Hullo, Brian, hullo, Sue. You know, when I was a small boy growing up in the East End of Baghdad, my old granny used to say, "War is a terrible thing unless you're on the winning side." And that's where I think *(cont'd. 94 kHz)*

© *BBC Radio War*

"This 24-hour rolling tapestry is getting me down"

Letters *to the Editor*

A Historic Boat Race

SIR – Your correspondent is incorrect in claiming that the famous "dead heat" of 1877 was the only occasion when the race was declared a "tie". There was an even more memorable (though now entirely forgotten) race in 1831 in which both boats simultaneously sank before reaching the starting line. My great-great-uncle, the Rev Winnifrith Hyde-Gussett (Eton and Balliol), later the Rural Dean of Hobart, where he published his classic treatise on the moths of Tasmania, was rowing stroke in the "Dark Blue" eight and would have drowned had it not been for the quick-witted intervention of Lord John Russell, who was watching the race from an upper window of the Star & Garter public house in Mortlake (now sadly demolished to make way for the local branch of The World Of Leather). The great statesman, who was at the time piloting the celebrated Great Reform Bill through the House of Commons, cast a handy wooden toilet seat into the river, just in time to save my distinguished relative from a watery grave. Floreat Oxonensia!
Sir Herbert Gussett
The Old Boat House,
Chorleywood.

● *The Editor thanks you for your communication but regrets that the Daily Telegraph no longer publishes this type of letter, on the instruction of their marketing consultants, Hargleby, Mandelson and Pratt, in the hope of attracting a younger readership. The preferred style is as follows:*

SIR – I hope the losing Cambridge crew are not feeling too "Light Blue" after their defeat!
Mike Giggler
(Via email)

'MILLIONAIRE' MAN FOUND GUILTY OF GREED

by Our Court Staff **Milly O'Nair**

IN A sensational climax to the three-month long "trial of the century", a judge yesterday described one of the leading participants as "a sad man motivated solely by greed, who would stop at nothing to become extraordinarily rich".

The judge continued: "Mr Chris Tarrant has for some years been systematically attempting to relieve television companies of huge sums of money, simply by sitting in a TV studio asking silly questions such as: "What is the capital of France? Is it a) Germany? b) Robbie Williams? c) The Long and Winding Road? or d) Grapefruit Segments?"

Turning his gaze on the guilty party, the judge said, "Mr Tarrant, not only have you displayed avarice of the highest order, but you and your co-conspirators in the Celador TV company have shamelessly encouraged large numbers of the public to lust obsessively after the chance of winning a million pounds.

"In all my years on the bench, I have never been confronted by such a shocking example of how human beings can be so degraded. I therefore sentence you to the greatest punishment I can conceive – namely to remain for the rest of your natural life incarcerated in Studio B, Teddington, asking your pitiful and absurd questions. And may the Lord have mercy on your soul.

"I turn, finally, to Major Ingram, an unfortunate victim of Mr Tarrant's hoax upon the public. Mr Ingram, you have patiently endured this farrago of a trial, sitting there in your regimental tie and agreeable blazer. As a member of our gallant armed forces who, even now, are bringing law and order to the streets of Basra, you have suffered enough. Case dismissed."

EX-ARMY OFFICER ACCUSED OF CHEATING

by Our Political Staff **Peter O'Bore**

A FORMER Army officer tried to bluff his way to becoming prime minister by an elaborate system of coughing whenever he was asked a question.

His scam was rumbled when television viewers saw the accused man, Captain Duncan Smith, nervously coughing whenever he was asked a question by quizmaster Tony Blair.

Who Wants To Be Completely Useless?

At one point Smith was asked to name the leader of the Tory Party and was given four choices: A. Michael Portillo; B. Kenneth Clarke; C. Sir Alec Douglas-Home; D. Oliver Letwin.

Videos clearly show Captain Smith looking deeply uncomfortable and coughing several times before asking whether he could phone a friend.

Unfortunately, he couldn't think of one, so the quizmaster moved on to ask: "In the current crisis over Iraq, who do you support? A. President Bush; B. President Saddam Hussein; C. President Blair; D. The late President Reagan."

After a long pause and a further prolonged bout of coughing, Captain Smith said, "I think it's D, but I can't be sure."

He was then arrested for fraud and for passing himself off as Leader of the Opposition.

● **Could you answer the questions which earned the Captain a million articles saying 'He's Not Up To It'?**

See our website –
www.duncansmith.cough.uk

ME AND MY SPOON

THIS WEEK

MAJOR CHARLES INGRAM

Would you describe the part played by spoons in your life as: a) Important, b) Not very important, c) Negligible, d) Seminal?

That is a tricky one. I'd probably say 'A' *(muted cough in the background)*. Er, on the other hand, it could be 'B'. Yes, I'll definitely plump for 'B' *(rather louder cough in the background)*. Ah, yes, I think perhaps I might reconsider that answer. I wonder how 'C' would go down? *(stupendous fit of coughing from back of room)* Oh, no, now I come to think about, it has to be 'D'. What was 'D' again? Oh yes, my final and definitive answer to your first question must be 'D'.

Has anything amusing ever happened to you in connection with a spoon?

Can I phone a friend?

NEXT WEEK: Clare Short – *"Me and My Shorts."*

GLENDA SLAGG

FLEET STREET'S ANSWER TO XXX!!?!?

■ SI SI! The Spanish will take El Becks and La Posho to their hearts when the sexy soccer icon goes a-prancin' and a-dancin' around the pitch in Madrid?!?! "Golé!" they'll shout (geddit?) at the top of their bullfighting voices when the Beautiful Game is played by the Beautiful Guy!?!? They'll go Really Mad-rid (geddit?!) for our Soccer Royalty, the Prince of Goals and the Princess of Spice!?!

■ TRAITOR!?! (And I don't mean George Galloway!?!?) That's the only word to describe the snivelling nancy-boy Beckham, who is skulking off to get his filthy hands on some Spanish Gold!?!? Gerroff – and take your skinny fashion victim of a wife and your kids with the silly names with you!?!? Go to El!?! (Geddit?!) The greasy paella-guzzling gauchos are welcome to you!?!?!

■ SEEN Liz Hurley's lips?!?!? OK, so she looks like something out of the Saatchi Gallery!?! Who cares!! She's still the loveliest gal in town – even if she does look like a trout that has had its lips blown up with a bicycle pump!

■ MAJOR Ingram – give that man a medal!?!? At least he had the guts to take on the greedy Chris Tarrant and the money-grubbing moguls of ITV?!?! OK, so he cheated!?! Who wouldn't in this day and age – especially when there's a million quid at stake!!?!

So hats off to the Major and his mad missus for the crazy coughin' that's given us something to smile about before we all die from SARS?!?!?

■ HERE THEY ARE – Glenda's May-Day Munchkins!?!

● **Tariq Aziz** – You can come and have a ziz round my place, big boy!?! And don't forget to bring round your weapon of mass destruction!?!?

● **Tecwen Whittock** – Crazy name, crazy cough!?!?

Byeeee!!!

Hated Arab Dictator Goes Into Exile

A Statement From Mohamed Al-Gnome

Many of you will have read the sad news that I have decided to go and live in Switzerland. I have been given no choice in this matter, due to the harsh and punitive tax regime operating in Britain, run by the Duke of Edinburgh.

I love this country and in the course of many years living here I have created jobs and opportunities for thousands of people in my shops: I have donated generously to charity and have recently rescued both Fugham FC and Punch magazine from obscurity.

And what is my fuggin reward? A final fuggin demand from the fuggin taxman for a billion pounds!

Well, my answer is this – fug off taxman, fug off the Duke of Edinburgh, Head of MI6, and fug off Britain. You know what you can do with your fuggin British passport. From now on I'm fuggin proud to be Swiss, with its wonderful cheese and no fuggin Royal Family...

Unfortunately, at this point, Mr Mohamed Al-Gnome was taken away by men in white coats believed to be bailiffs.

Notes & Queries

QUESTION: Who invented the "Jiffy Bag"?

☐ MRS D. RUMSFELD is quite wrong in claiming that the Jiffy Bag was invented by an employee of the Pittsburgh Packaging Company in 1873. As surely everybody knows, this useful postal device was in fact the brainchild of a Belgian tax-collector and amateur entomologist, Maximilien Jiffé (1841-97), who filled envelopes with horsehair to protect specimens of moths he had collected in the jungles of the Belgian Congo in order to send them back to the Institute Papillionistique in Limoges. The now-familiar "bubble wrap" design was developed in the 1950s by two Canadian scientists, Hal J. Bubble and Jean-Jacques Wrap, whose company, The Bubble Wrap Corporation of Ontario, was later taken over by the Belgian multi-national Jiffé. Hence the "Jiffy" Bag, or – more properly – the "Jiffé" Bag. **Horace Nicholson**, author of *It'll Be There In A Jiffy! – The True Story Of The Jiffy Bag* (Short Books, £7.99).

QUESTION: Does anyone know the origin of the popular expression "Get a life"?

☐ THIS now-famous phrase was the slogan of an advertising campaign in the mid-1950s to launch a new brand of cigarettes called "Life". Cinema and TV commercials showed the young Ronald Reagan as a cowboy, pulling a cigarette from his holster and saying "Get a Life!" to a pretty young Indian squaw (played by Gina Lollobrigida). The end of the film showed them fondly embracing, each holding a "Life" cigarette. The campaign was a commercial disaster and the new brand was discontinued after only three weeks. **Dr Vijay Fotherington-Thomas**, Mumbai.

Answers, please, to the following: Can frogs yawn? Is it true that the crossword was invented in Mesopotamia? Is David Frost still alive?

SADDAM RESTAURANT SHOCK

Who ordered the bombe surprise?

The amusing sayings of Iraq's hysterical new funster – Said-al Sahaf!

THE laugh-a-minute Iraqi Minister for Information has tickled the ribs of the world with his electrodes (*surely amusing asides, Ed*) and has kept the west laughing in the dark days of the war.

Here is a selection of his hilarious one liners.

● *"The only good Kurd is a dead Kurd."*

● *"Take these people away to be tortured."*

● *"Shoot them all and bury them in a pit."*

©*All newspapers*

I AM THERE AS WAR ENDS

by Our Man In The Palestine Hotel **I.I.I. Mee**

AS the Abrahams Tanks rumbled along the open highway into Baghdad I stood and watched them with my own eyes. When the first battalion of the Kentucky Fried Marines led by Colonel Sanders (*subs: can you check this please?*) arrived in the main square I saw them personally out of my hotel window.

And when the statue of Saddam Hussein finally toppled to the ground it was me who witnessed it.

Yes, throughout the war the story has been the same – I was there.

Today an elderly Iraqi man embraced me in the street weeping profusely and handing me a garland of flowers, "Thank Allah that you are here," he cried. "A thousand blessings on you for coming to rescue us."

And the US military were equally grateful. A young American soldier, Corporal Ronald McDonald from the elite Taco Bell Rangers (*subs:*

check again please), shook my hand saying, "It is an honour and a privilege to be the first member of the coalition forces to meet you, sir."

Luckily, the world's photographers were on hand to capture this defining image of the entire war against Saddam – me, standing in front of the fallen statue, hitting it with my shoe.

When the dust has settled, when the history books come to be written, and when I place my grandchildren on my knee, I will be able to tell them with pride – that yes, I was there.

© *All Hacks who were there.*

BUSH'S PEACE PLAN FOR ULSTER

by Our Northern Irish Staff **General Stormont Normont**

PRESIDENT BUSH flew into Belfast yesterday to be greeted by crowds of cheering policemen who were on double-overtime.

Said the President: "I am delighted to be here in Belfastland, the home of the shamrock and the bonny leprechaun.

"I bring you today a message of peace. For too long your country has suffered under the tyranny of the terrorists, known as the IRAQ, under their hated leader Mr Gerry Saddams.

"But I am here to tell these folks that they may run, but there is no

hiding place. They must give up their weapons of mass destruction, their Semtex, their agricultural fertiliser and their nuclear weapons.

"Failing that, they must expect the full wrath of the Coalition forces, as we send in the finest armed forces in the world to liberate the Irish people and allow them to rejoin the world community."

At this point, Mr Bush was interrupted by Tony Blair, who thanked him for his kind remarks and led him over to meet his friends Mr Adams and Mr McGuinness.

"I shall name you 'Good Friday'"

IRAQ WAR
An Apology

IN THE PAST three weeks, we at the BBC may have inadvertently given the impression through all our outlets that the Allied incursion into Iraq was militarily ill-conceived in every respect and unsupported by the Iraqi people, who regarded it as a ruthless invasion of their sacred homeland, and which was certain to end in total disaster. News headlines such as "Coalition Bogged Down In New Vietnam", "Baghdad Will Be Worse Than Stalingrad", "Blundering Coalition Forces On Brink Of Humiliating Defeat By Saddam's Super-Elite Special Republican Guard" may have given the impression that we believed in some way that the war was not going quite as well as planned.

In the light of recent events, we now accept – albeit with a very bad grace – that the coalition forces seem for the time being to have got away with it, and that large numbers of Iraqis, though clearly paid by the CIA to do so, may have appeared to be not entirely displeased at the downfall of a regime which, whatever its faults, did at least for 30 years guarantee the stability of a potentially explosive mix of Shias, Sunnis and Kurds, who will now undoubtedly plunge the whole region into a state of chaos which will threaten the peace of the world.

Whilst apologising for any confusion to which our reports may have given rise (and allowing for the fact that they could be broadcast only under monitoring restrictions imposed by the Iraqi authorities), we now realise that the only hope for future peace is for the hated Bush/Blair imperialist aggressors to be replaced at once by a French-led UN force of Russian troops of the type who were so successful in bringing peace to the Muslims of Groszny.

© The BBC (and Channel Four)

A Camel Driver Writes

Each week a well-known Arab commentator is asked to give his views on the state of the war.

THIS WEEK: **Saladin al-Nuttah** (Camel No. 341273)

See them Iraqis, guv? What a shower! Call themselves Arabs?! First shot fired in anger and they run up the white flag! Makes you ashamed to wear a moustache! Blimey! And then they go round lootin' all that stuff out the shops and that – even stealin' from sick kiddies in hospital and that! I don't know what the Arab world is coming to! That Saddam Hussein had the right idea – string 'em up! It's the only language they understand.

I had that John Simpson on the back of my camel once. Camel gave up halfway to the airport. Very heavy man.

© All newspapers in Egypt, Syria, Jordan, Palestine, North London etc.

Those Israeli Elections In Full

(Cont. from p. 1)

ARMAGEDDON CENTRAL.

Ariel Atak (Some Likud Hot Party) 30,816; **General Smitem Buldoza** (They Don't Likud Up Them Party) 29,405; **Rabbi Looni Ben Nutkase** (No Trousers On The Sabbath Party) 13,402; **Barbara Amiel** (Daily Tel Aviv Party) 2,307; **Softi Ben Neissman** (Labour Let's Be Kind To Palestinians Alliance) 0.

BETHLEHEM EAST. No change.

Election cancelled due to absence of Electorate. (That's enough elections. Ed.)

WHO WILL RUN POST-WAR IRAQ?
Those top candidates in full

Mr Shufti Cruki (59) Charismatic Iraqi exile and chairman of the sadly defunct Cruki Bank of Jordan. Supremely able, Cruki is the first choice of the US State Department.

Ayatollah Ma'ad Mahdi (63) Charismatic Islamic fundamentalist leader of the powerful Complete Shi'ite Faction. Supremely mad, he is the sworn enemy of (see below)

Ayatollah Sunni An-Cher (73) Charismatic Islamic fundamentalist leader of the minority Sunni Delight Faction. Supremely dead due to being hacked to death by the above…

General Jed Bush (no relation) (63) Uncharismatic idiot who has no idea where Iraq is.

Saddam Hussein (73) Charismatic strongman and chairman of the Baa'staad Party who aims to restore *(cont p.94)*

BAGHDAD Loot

For sale

● **Heart monitor**, hardly used, $10 o.n.o Apply Ali. Ref 1496.

● **3rd century Sumerian alabaster head**, possibly Shalman Rushdee III, $7. Apply Mohammed. Ref 7342.

● **Filing cabinet**, ex-Ministry of Information, some files missing, $22. Apply Saddam (no relation, honestly). Ref 8993.

● **Weapons of mass destruction**, guaranteed genuine, authenticated by D. Rumsfeld (no relation) or possibly fridge, $3.29, buyer collect. Apply Assif. Ref 3783

More inside

NEW OUTBREAK OF SARIS

MORE victims shown here of the mysterious Eastern disease that strikes middle-aged Westerners who want to suck-up to the Asian community.

WHAT THE PAPERS SAY

"Words can't describe the sublime way Vermeer has depicted the earthenware in this masterpiece."
The Times

"Nice jugs!"
The Sun

Are you a victim of the killer flu?

10 Tell Tale Signs That You Could Be The Victim of the World's Most Deadly New Disease

1. You are Chinese.
2. You've got a headache and a runny nose.
3. You're wearing a Michael Jackson-style face mask.
4. The Rolling Stones have cancelled a concert near your home.
5. There's a picture of you on the front page of the *Daily Mail* under the headline "House Prices Tumble as Killer Flu strikes Britain".
6. You're dead.
7. ...er...
8. ...that's it.

Which Top Fleet Street Doc Would You Want To Tell You That You've Got The Chinese Killer?

═ YOU CHOOSE ═

Dr James Le Fanu
1. Rides bike.
2. Heavy smoker.
3. Writes for *Telegraph*.

Dr Thomas Stuttaford
1. Was Tory MP.
2. Likes his wine.
3. Writes for *Times*.

Ring our special Sars "Doc-line" now, and help decide which of these media medics is the nation's favourite!!!
0896-4141300 (calls £1 a minute)

The Paul Getty Who Knew Me

by **Dominic Lawson** (aged 12)

I shall never forget going on Paul Getty's yacht. It was really big, and really impressed all the locals when we anchored in some flash Mediterranean harbour.

His was always the biggest boat there, and you could have drinks on it and everything.

The story that I think best sums up my very good friend (and one of the world's richest men) was when, one night, we were all drinking this fabulously expensive French wine.

He turned to me in the middle of dinner and said, "Who are you?".

It showed how full of curiosity this man was about his fellow human beings. I shall never forget it.

© D. Lawson *The Sunday Gettygraph*

The Paul Getty Who Knew Me

by **Sir John Rumpole** (aged 94)

I shall never forget the many fabulous parties I was asked to at Sir Paul Getty's enormous estate.

Fortunately, it was quite near where I live in the Chilterns, so one didn't have to drive too far to get there. But it was certainly worth it, for the chance to sample Paul's legendary cellar.

The story that I think best sums him up was the time when, in the middle of lunch, I leaned over to him and asked, "Could I have another glass of that excellent champagne?"

Without a word he filled my glass to the brim. That's how he was, generous to the end.

© Sir J. Rumpole

New Words Enter Dictionary

THE LATEST edition of the Longman dictionary of contemporary English includes a number of new entries which reflect the contemporary urban speech of modern Britain. Here are some of the hottest words on the street that have now officially entered the English language.

■ **Toasta** *(noun)* electrical appliance used for grilling bread. Derived from Afro-Caribbean youth patois.

■ **Retchin** *(adj.)* cool, hip, happening, trendy, out-of-date, old-fashioned, embarrassing *(see also Bling Blong)*.

■ **Spang** *(noun)* good-looking member of the opposite sex wearing an orange-hooded garment *(see Twag)*.

■ **Trouza press** *(noun)* urban criminal gang involved in the laundering of gentlemen's garments.

■ **Boguzz** *(noun)* type of popular contemporary music, a fusion of garage, trip hop, trance, bungla, rip rap, plop, daddy, mood, weenie and peregrine worsthorne.

■ **Sillee** *(noun)* desperate attempt by dictionary publisher to get into newspaper.

■ **Phatuous** *(adj.)* unlikely word you've never heard of now included in sillee dictionary.

(That's enough new words. Ed.)

RUSSELL CROWE WEDDING

> You may now kick the photographer

Are You Looking For A Bonding Weekend?

Why not try The Old Thatchery, Berks?

All facilities are available, including:

■ Conference Room big enough to seat entire party (25) ■ Blue Sky Brainstorming Room with video facilities and giant poster of David Mellor ■ Trouser Press for those casual jeans ■ Bad Press for your useless ideas ■ Mini Bar for drinking to forget that your leader is IDS and not William Hague ■ Heated Swimming Pool for Barrymore-style ending to problems.

Book now to avoid disappointment!

☙ THE INDEPENDENT

Friday 2 May 2003

WHY DOES the Independent keep filling the front page with questions in big type? *Hasn't it got any stories?* Can't it afford any photographs? What about a drawing? Or is that too expensive as well? **And what about that front page full of numbers?** *What was that all about?* Isn't that enough? Ed.

*"Actually, it's a Tory **bonding** weekend"*

THE DAILY TELEGRAPH

How We Got The Scoop Of The Millennium

by Charles 'Scoop' Moore

Editor of the
Daily Telegraph

EVERYONE in the world is talking about our amazing scoop!

Well, now I'm going to reveal how we did it.

The Telegraph's top reporter in Baghdad, William Boot, was wandering past the war-shattered Ministry of Secrets when he noticed a door open.

He walked in and found a scene of total chaos. Looting mobs had stripped the entire building bare.

Only one room remained miraculously intact.

There, surrounded by smoke-blackened rubble, was a small cardboard box bearing the legend, in Arabic, "For the attention of the Daily Telegraph".

Feverishly tearing the box open, our man found, to his astonishment, a pile of perfectly preserved documents marked "Ultra Top Secret – For Saddam's Eyes Only" (also in Arabic).

Boot at once suspected that he had stumbled unexpectedly on a sensational scoop – nothing less than the "smoking gun" that would prove beyond any doubt that the war had not been a waste of time.

The first priceless find was a letter from Sir Edward Heath, offering to conduct the Baghdad Radio Symphony Orchestra in exchange for an appropriate fee (300,000 barrels of oil).

Next was a letter from the Rev. J.C. Flannel, vicar of St Ivel's church in Neasden, enclosing a cheque for £5.53 collected at a special Evensong For Peace, made out to "The Victims of the Allied Sanctions Regime".

But the greatest prize of all was nestling at the bottom of the box – nothing less than a signed letter from Saddam Hussein himself, promising Labour MP George Galloway control of the entire Kirkuk oil field as "a small token of our appreciation for your articles in the Mail on Sunday (Scottish edition), describing Mr Blair as a 'worse war criminal' than Hitler. PS.

Incidentally, Hitler was a good man!"

The letter was signed in Mr Hussein's absence by the head of his elite Medina Letter-Writing Division, whose name was illegible.

There could be no more solid proof than this that George Galloway should be hanged for treason – if indeed he is guilty, as our lawyers have asked me to add, and which of course he was last night vehemently denying from his luxury £250,000 Algarve hideaway.

On Other Pages

Gorgeous George's Sultry Palestinian Wife – Is She More Lovely Than Liz? (Pics and comments by Alexander Chancellor.)

The Daily Telegraph
Bring him to justice

DESPITE the liberation of Iraq, our readers know that the war isn't over until the mustachioed tyrant is finally brought to justice. And that man of course is George Galloway *(surely 'Saddam Hussein'? Ed)*.

If it is proved that a third country, such as Portugal *(surely 'Syria'? Ed)* is harbouring this dangerous despot, then Washington has no choice but to invade Europe to flush this evil lunatic from his bolthole *(now you're talking. Ed)*.

Telegraph Exclusive

This Week's Incredible Document Discoveries

SUNDAY

Confidential, top secret letter found in Ministry of Foreign Affairs, dated 3rd March 2003, from President Chirac of France, offering Saddam a chateau in the Loire Valley, a seat in his cabinet and the use of his wife should he desire it at any point. Signed *"Votre cher ami, Jacques"* in Arabic.

WEDNESDAY

Confidential secret letter found in Ministry of Weapons of Mass Destruction, dated April 1st 2003, from President Putin of Russia, offering to supply Saddam Hussein with as many nuclear weapons as he would like at "a very reasonable price". Signed, *"Your Comrade-in-Arms against the forces of American imperialism, Vladimir Stalin"* in Arabic.

FRIDAY

Confidential, top secret, thank you letter to Saddam Hussein found in Ministry of Unburnt Documents, dated April 15th 2003, from Osama bin Laden.

It says, *"A thousand thank yous for the plane and the towers idea. It worked a treat. Here's to the next time!"* Your Jihad Co-warrior against the Infidel Osama bin Laden.

SUNDAY

Confidential, top secret letter, dated May 2nd 2003, to Saddam Hussein from the editor of the Daily Mail in which he thanks Saddam for helping to bring down house prices and hasten the downfall of the hated Tony Blair. It is signed *"Your brother against the New Labour dictatorship, Paul Dacre,"* in Arabic. (*That's enough secret documents. Ed.*)

Lives of the Saints
St George of England

Gorgeous St George

THE LEGEND of St George is shrouded in mystery, but the familiar story has been handed down to believers and is one we still revere today – how the noble George of Galloway bravely took on the Daily Telegraph and slew the monster in an epic battle in the High Court.

George is traditionally depicted as a hero standing alone against the fire-breathing, right-wing newspaper.

There are, of course, other scurrilous versions of the legend in which St George emerges in a less flattering light – namely, as a bit of a shifty self-publicist. In one variation of the tale, St George is actually defeated by the dragon and executed for treason.

But today we celebrate the enduring popular myth of the great English hero St George, with his red cross face and his trusty moustache *(cont. p. 94)*

Taken from the Book of English Martyrs by St Christopher the Sylvester.

60

POLLY FILLER

On Post-War Iraq

THE pictures on the television of the battered and looted city of Baghdad tell the tragic story of a nation on the brink. With law and order collapsing, typhoid breaking out and religious fundamentalism on the rise, how on earth can sanity prevail? Well, to anyone looking at the scenes of all those men behaving badly(!), the solution is glaringly obvious. Put a woman in charge! And not just *any* woman, but the sort of busy career woman who is already juggling her work and her home life, her job and her family. Any woman who can organise a football birthday cake for the toddler, whilst paying off the Barclaycard bill and taking a conference call

from the boss can easily handle something as simple as restoring normality to Iraq.

As the heroine of my best-selling novel *Mummy For Old Rope*, Jilly Fuller, puts it, "If a job's worth doing, it's worth getting a woman to do it properly."

My post bag is full of letters from women all over the world saying that Jilly Fuller is an international role model who could make the world a better place – as well as making a packed lunch for the school trip to the Science Museum! And that's what I've learned from Jilly Fuller, the heroine of my best-selling book *Mummy For Old Rope*. When the chips are down (or rather, in the oven with the dinoburgers, ready for feeding an army of boisterous urchins who have come round after Chess Club!), you don't want to rely on the Useless Simons of this world to get anything done.

Because, instead of reconnecting the public utilities, the Baghdad Simons are probably watching Celebrity 4x4 Fox Hunting with Jeremy Clarkson and A.A. Gill on Al-Jazeera Extreme Sport!

No! What's called for in Iraq is clearly what my readers describe as "a Jilly Fuller moment". You know – when the hard-pressed executive mum saves the day with an ice-cream and a smiley-faced sticking plaster

whilst closing a multi-million pound deal, moving home and hiring a new nanny from Zimbabwe!

TALKING of which, why have I got through 11 au pairs in as many weeks? You give these girls a fantastic opportunity to learn English for 20 minutes a day whilst driving the toddler to nursery school and then they complain about the odd 12 hours a night ironing Simon's underpants!!

And please(!) spare us the sob story about your village being burnt to the ground! One of your relatives was probably just having a furtive fag (like you do in the downstairs loo!).

Even I take a tip from Jilly Fuller, the heroine of my best-selling book *Mummy For Old Rope*. In the much-praised opening chapter, Jilly confronts her hopeless Rwandan au pair and quips "You're like your village back in Africa. Sacked!"

So, Mr Bush and Mr Blair, if you are reading this column (as my sources tell me you do regularly do!), enough of this half-hearted dithering and take some decisive action. Send for Jilly Fuller, heroine of my best-selling novel *Mummy For Old Rope*.

© Polly Filler.

● *Polly Filler's novel* Mummy For Old Rope *is out now in paperback, published by Pearson Macdonald, price £7.99.*

TV Highlights

The 100 Cheapest Television Programmes
C4, 9.00pm

Which Channel 4 programme will top the poll and win the title of Cheapest TV Programme Of All Time?

Will it be 100 Greatest Film Stars? Or 100 Greatest Weather Girls? Or 100 Greatest Clips of Johnny Vegas talking about the 100 Greatest List Programmes He's Been On?

Join Channel Four for an evening guaranteed not to cost very much *(Surely "to keep the nation glued to its seats"? Ed.).*

Tabloid Tales
BBC1, 10.35pm

Presented by Piers Morgan. Morgan looks at victims of the press who have been involved in major scandals. Tonight he interviews himself about the sharedealing scam that nearly ended his career and asks himself whether the press was really to blame or whether it was actually all his own fault and he was incredibly lucky not to be fired and then prosecuted by the DTI.

"It's not as good as Teacher's"

The Sunday Times Pretty Rich List

1. **Rupert Murdoch** Pretty rich of him to publish a list of the filthy rich without putting himself in it.

2. **The Sunday Times** Pretty rich of them to leave out the details of their

owner's enormous wealth and include everyone else's.

3. Er...

4. That's rich.

"Ralph's preparing them for their new secondary school, apparently it's quite rough"

2003 National Curriculum Tests

Question 7

If the Government goes ahead with plans to make all seven and eleven-year-olds sit this test will your teacher…

A   Go on strike after lunch break?

B   Go on strike at the end of the day?

C   Go on strike tomorrow?

D   None of the above as he's already on strike over teaching assistants being allowed to take some classes?

Today Programme Wins Top 'Tony Award'

by Our Media Staff **Ray D. O'Four**

THE Radio 4 morning current affairs programme *Toady* yesterday picked up the top "Oscar" of the radio world.

The Tony Awards are given to broadcasters who have excelled themselves in sucking up to the government and this year the judges were unanimous in giving John Humphrys the overall prize for his coverage of the local elections.

"The *Toady* programmes managed not to mention that Labour had lost," said the judges' citation, "and instead focused on the fact that the Tories had only won a dismal most of the vote and a disappointing huge increase in seats."

ZETA-JONES BABY

We're going to call her Sue

"It's so realistic! Imagine an internet chat-room with interactive 3D graphics!"

"A question from the gentleman at the back – yes, you sir, in the cardinal's hat"

What You Missed

THE ARTS DOCUMENTARY OF THE MILLENNIUM

Yentob

Presented by Leonardo Da Vinci

(Dramatic music)

Leonardo Da Vinci *(for it is he)*: No one can deny the extraordinary genius of the man known simply to generations of art lovers as "Yentob".

(Enter actor dressed as world-famous BBC Head of something-or-other.)

Da Vinci: Alano da Yentob was a true Renaissance Man. Not only could he sit in pointless management meetings...

(Dramatic reconstruction shows actor shuffling papers marked "Internal Resource Directorate".)

Da Vinci: ...but he could also commission himself to present flagship arts documentaries.

(Reconstruction shows actor talking to reflection in mirror.)

Yentob *(to mirror)*: Who on earth can I get to front this major series?

Yentob *(in mirror)*: How about myself?

Yentob: What a brilliant idea.

You are a genius.

Yentob: And so am I.

(More dramatic music.)

Leonardo: Yes, the world of the arts was never going to be the same again. But Yentob was also an inventor, the creator of a number of revolutionary vehicles like 'The Omnibus'. But did it actually work?

(We see dramatic reconstruction of Yentob interviewing Mel Brooks.)

Yentob: Ha ha ha ha, Mel. You're really wonderful!

Da Vinci: It certainly worked for him, but sadly Yentob was not taken seriously in his own time. Even his most enduring legacy, the sublime 'Last of the Supper Wine', was not sufficiently admired by his contemporaries and it is only today that we can fully appreciate the extraordinary range of talent that made up the man we know as the all-powerful BBC Head of Paperclips Leonardo da Botney *(That's quite enough. Ed.)*

THIS WEEK

RT REV ROWAN WILLIAMS
Archbishop of Canterbury

Do you see spoons as having a moral dimension?

What I think we need to clarify is the position of spoons in the overall context of cutlery generally. Why should we particularise spoons, as you have done, when knives and forks may be equally valid? What we should be doing is factoring into this equation a wider and deeper awareness of the ethical significance of the spoon issue in all its implications...

...er, do you like spoons?

Your question poses a further question in the way it is formulated. Do we have a compelling strategy for confronting a problem of this nature, where what is paramount is a persuasive theory of a new energy rooted in our experience of the spoon as a useful adjunct to the minutiae of our everyday existence? And I think you'll agree that one cannot express it more clearly than that.

...er, has anything amusing ever happened to you in connection with a spoon?

Can we reconcile the conflicting imperatives of that which can be considered conceptually amusing with the perhaps more concrete, albeit mundane physicality of the spoon taken as an object which...

...thank you, Archbishop.

NEXT WEEK: Michael Portillo – *"Me and My Pillow."*

The Tony Blair I Don't Remember Very Well

by Fellow Oxford Undergraduate From The Class Of '72, **Geoff Beard**

TONY BLAIR and I were never friends and probably never met, but I do remember standing in the queue for lunch at St John's College and seeing a bloke in front of me who was wearing flared trousers and had long hair. He had pie, chips and beans as I recall, but I don't think it was him.

The Tony Blair I Don't Remember Either

by **Colin Bald**

THAT first day at St John's will for ever be etched in my memory. I was standing in the Beer Cellar having a pint with my fellow tutees when in came this extraordinary figure holding a guitar and wearing a boater. He had charisma, style and charm. The girls all loved him.

I should have known even then that one day he would end up as Creative Director of the advertising agency Bogleby Bowtie and Pratt. He was, of course, Martin Bowtie and apparently he once met Tony Blair.

The Tony Blair Who I Don't Remember Coming To Any Meetings Of The Far Left Caucus

by **Dave Spart**

ER... basically, the sickening truth is that whilst I and my comrades from St John's were illegally occupying the laundry room in a sit-in protest against the totally fascist overcharging for the use of the tumble-dryer machine er... the proto Conservative Tony so-called Blair was typically nowhere to be seen or he might have been there, but I can't remember *(Cont. p. 94)*

TONY BLAIR: HOW HE HAS AGED

Tony in 1997

Tony now

O GEORGE HAMILTON
O JUDITH CHALMERS
O DAVID DICKINSON

CLARE SHORT QUITS 'REALITY HELL'

by Our TV Staff **Phil Screen**

Disturbing scene from last night's show

A TEAR-stained Clare Short last night decided to leave the long-running TV reality show *'I'm A Liability Get Me Out Of Here'*.

The popular programme is set in the jungle of Westminster and features a group of B-list MPs who have to undertake various challenges to stay in the "Government".

Clare Short had to undergo "the creepy-crawly challenge" in which she had to "creepy-crawl" up Mr Blair's bottom.

Taken Short

"I just couldn't do it," she sobbed, "even though the others seemed to have no trouble completing the task."

She continued, "It is all too humiliating and my fellow contestants really got on my nerves. That David with a beard was far too bossy and tried to control everyone. I hated the gay one, Mandy, too, who whined and whinged all the time. And as for Tessa Jowell... she'll flirt with anyone just to stay in."

Clare de Loon

Clare follows other high profile non-entities to leave the show, including the bearded TV Cook Robin and the deeply disturbed Welsh badger lover Ron Davies *(cont. p. 94)*

'I'M A CELEBRITY GET ME OUT OF HERE'

It's The TV Programme That Everyone's Talking About –

Read The Exclusive Highlights Only In Private Eye TV 2 Digital

9.15am Live

Man with beard: I'm going to get some logs now.

Other man: Yeah, get some logs. Good idea. Logs. That's what we need.

Blonde woman: Sob.

Other blonde woman: Sob.

Man with hat on: Need a hand with those logs?

(Cut to two small boys on bridge)

Ant (or possibly Dec): Who do you think should do the log challenge? The man with the beard? The other man? Or the man in the hat?

Dec (or possibly Ant): Or should it be the blonde who's sobbing? Or what about the sobbing blonde?

Ant/Dec: Ring 017532146789...

Dec/Ant: ...423576075324

9.17am Live

(Cut back to man with beard)

Man with beard: I've got the logs.

Other man: Good. Great. Logs.

Blonde woman: Sob.

(Continued for 94 hours)

From the pen that brought you Heir Of Sorrows and La Dame Aux Camillas

BORN TO BE QUEENY

The Love Story that dare not speak its name

by SYLVIE KRIN

TONY AND GORDON are trapped in a loveless relationship. Matters are complicated by Tony's old partner, Peter, whose constant interference creates an impossible triangle of seething passions and irreconcilable emotions.

Now read on...

"WE CAN'T go on like this, Gordon." The tall, good-looking, tousle-haired Prime Minister was standing by the window of his elegant drawing room, lit up by the pink rays of a gorgeous London sunset.

On the wall behind him, a gilt-framed portrait of Mrs Thatcher at her most commanding looked down on the two men, who were standing at opposite ends of the room, eyeing each other suspiciously.

"You're still seeing him, aren't you, Tony?" said the saturnine, dark-haired, Byronic Chancellor of the Exchequer. "They tell me you talk to each other every day."

Tony tossed his head petulantly.

"What if I do? And what business is it of yours, anyway?"

The brooding wizard of finance mopped his brow with a lilac handkerchief as he allowed himself to speak frankly of his innermost torment.

"And they're talking about us, Tony. They're saying we can't stop rowing."

"That's not *my* fault, is it?" snapped the boyish, yet fast-ageing, hero of Baghdad.

"Yes it is!"

"No it isn't!"

"Yes it is!"

The bitter, staccato recriminations of the two men were broken into by the melodious ringing of a pink mobile phone from the top drawer of Tony's presidential desk.

"Go on, Tony, answer it. It's him, isn't it? Go ahead and talk to him. You know you want to."

"It's not who you think it is, Gordon."

"Then why is it playing YMCA?"

Tony blushed, as he stepped forward to answer the only-too-familiar ring.

"Look," he murmured into the mouthpiece with a look of embarrassment. "I can't talk now. Certain people are in the room... of course I'm talking to him... he's my friend... Gordon and I go back a long way... Look, Peter, that's not very nice... I don't want to hear that sort of thing...

that's not worthy of you, Peter... Goodbye – and I mean goodbye."

Tony threw the phone back into the drawer and slammed it shut.

There was an uneasy silence as the eyes of the two men met across the room.

"Thank you, Tony," Gordon was the first to speak. "I appreciate what you just did. And you're right, you and I do go back a long, long way..."

His voice trembled with repressed emotion.

"I'm sorry, Gordon. I've been under a lot of stress lately. You know, the war, the Olympic bid, bloody Clare Short – now, there *is* a bitch!"

The two men laughed spontaneously, with a warmth that they hadn't shown each other for years.

"What fools we've been!" said Tony, seizing the moment. "I know – let's have a party, to tell the world that we really are together again..."

"WE really are together again! You can take my word for it." The table of admiring lady journalists, gathered in the fashionable Knightsbridge restaurant La Hacketta, hung on Peter's every word.

"Tony and I have never been closer," he assured the fastest-rising stars of the political journalistic firmament.

They gazed at him adoringly – Anne Applejuice, Sarah Sandcastle, Rachel Silly, Anne McElvoid, Mary-Ann Siegfriedsassoon.

Anything that was passed on in strictest confidence to these influential commentators was certain to be all over the front pages next morning – as he well knew!

"Tony's a lovely man, but he takes his eye off the ball." The sultry Sultan of Spin smiled his shy smile, and arched his eyebrows.

"Now this must go no further, it really mustn't! You'd be very naughty girls if a word of it was ever to appear in your papers."

He took a long meaningful sip of his favourite Brazilian liqueur, Ole Marineros, before delivering his *coup de grace*.

"Gordon's been running rings round Tony recently. But then you knew that, didn't you? I feel so sorry for Tony. You just can't let him out on his own! It's a good thing he's got at least one real friend who's there to pick up the pieces."

Peter winked knowingly at the tableful of women, all scribbling furiously into their notebooks...

The Greatest Englishman Since The Duke of Wellington

by Sir William Really-Smugg
The Greatest Living Columnist

I was spending an agreeable weekend in the West Country, surrounded by seven generations of Really-Smuggs. They ranged from my two-year-old great-great nephew, who has just got into Oxford, to my 103-year-old self. Inevitably, the subject turned to the greatest Englishman of this and perhaps any other time, David Beckham, known to his millions of fans as "Posh".

For those of my readers who are unfamiliar with the achievements of Mr Beckham, as I am, let me explain that he is a popular footballer, who plays for a club in the north of England known as Manchester Rovers. Apparently, he is adored by millions of our fellow countrymen and women, from all walks of life, young and old, black and white, Protestant and Catholic, dustmen and dukes, gays and straights.

One would need to go back to the days of Admiral Nelson to find any young Englishmen more admired throughout the country. And before him who? One thinks perhaps of King Henry V leading his "team" onto the "pitch" at Agincourt. Mr Beckham would not have looked out of place, urging on his "lads" with a cry of "God for Fergie, England and Saint George Best".

Here in the leafy lanes of Somerset, as Spring burgeons from every hedgerow, the name of "Beckham" seems to be on the lips of the very birds themselves, from the humble chiff-chaff to the great Somerset Tit, myself.

© **Lord Really-Smugg 1803.**

"From here you can see six asylum centres"

McLACHLAN

Why I Am Not William Deedes

by William Boot

Extracts from "Shurely Shome Mishtake – the Real Shtory of Shcoop" by William F. Boot.

I FIRST met Bill Deedes in Abyssinia just before the Coronation of Haile Satirical, the Ethiopian Potentate, in the summer of 1827. I was sharing a tent in the middle of the desert with the legendary American correspondent, J.J. Knickerbocker-Glory III, known to his intimates as "Johnny" Trouserpress.

We were drinking Pimms and discussing England's chances of winning the Test when in walked this extraordinary figure wearing a three-piece suit, a top hat and spats. "Good evening," he said in the manner that was to become familiar to millions of readers when he was immortalised in the novel "Mr Deedes Goes to the Daily Telegraph".

Deedes must have been at least 94, but he had the agility of mind of a man of 107.

TOMORROW: *Why I am not Evelyn Waugh.*

SAATCHI GALLERY OPENS

I don't know much about arse but I know what I like

At the Movies with JOHNNY HYPE

THE MATRIX REGURGITATED

THIS IS a fab film because it must be. Everyone says so. And never before has any movie spent so much money on sending me press releases saying how great it is. Which proves it! Everywhere you look there are spectacular adverts for it and big pieces about it in the newspapers. So it *has* to be brilliant! And I'm hardly going to stick my neck out and say that actually it's the same old stuff except not as good this time round, am I? That's hardly going to get my quote on the poster is it? No, this is "a high-octane, 100-megadrive, pulse-raising, kick-ass, kung-fu action, sci-fi adventure, philosophical thriller whodunnit" *Johnny Hype, The Daily Drivel*. It gets the full five stars from the Johnny Hype column but then so do all the films!!

Hype rating ★★★★★

★	Absolutely fantastic
★★	Really brilliant and great
★★★	Big goody bag
★★★★	Premiere tickets
★★★★★	Invite to Cannes

65

The Times Souvenir Edition

50 Years On – The Day No One Will Ever Remember

The Times is privileged to print in advance a facsimile of its special edition to mark the Coronation of King Charles III

THE  TIMES

SMALL CROWDS FAIL TO CHEER AS NEW KING IS CROWNED

LONDON SUNSHINE FAILS TO KINDLE ENTHUSIASM

From Our Special Correspondent

As London basked in warm June sunlight, a handful of foreign tourists stood outside Westminster Abbey yesterday to watch the arrival of the elderly King Charles, 100, and his venerable consort, Her Royal Highness Mrs Parker-Bowles, as they climbed out of the Golden Mini-Cab for an informal coronation ceremony, sponsored by Vodafone.

The new-style service, personally devised by the King himself, along with the Archbishop of Canterbury, Mrs Sylvia Onanugu, and the Dean of Westminster, Imam Osama bin Hussein, lasted 20 minutes and incorporated elements of all the world's major religions, except Christianity.

DAY TO FORGET

As the Royal couple walked up the aisle with the aid of their gilt zimmer frames, designed by the King's talented nephew, Lord Linley, they were welcomed by representatives of the King's favourite causes, including:
● the British Society of Watercolourists
● Friends of the Level Crossing
● the Save The House Sparrow Society
● Bring Back Shakespeare Trust

Among the sparse congregation of foreign dignitaries were President Blair of the United States of Europe, President Chelsea Clinton of the USA, and the Grand Zlog of the Martian Republic.

Among those too busy to attend the ceremony were: HRH the Prince William, HRH the Princess Anne not accompanied by one of her many husbands, and Lord Romeo Beckham, Red Shirt Pursuivant and Master of the Royal Tattoos.

After the ceremony, the King laid a wreath on the Tomb of the Unknown Organic Farmer who gave his life at the battle of Monsanto in the great GM wars of the early 21st Century.

As the King was confirmed by the Health and Safety Executive as a "competent person to act as monarch", a choir from St Paul McCartney's Fame Academy performed the anthem "Nul Points".

The King and his wife then made their way to the Westminster Tube Station, accompanied by a team of social workers from the First Battalion of the Household Cavalry.

They then made an appearance on the balcony of their 28th floor flat in the Gordon Brown Tower, Canary Wharf, to witness a fly-past of Lord Branson's "Moon And Back In A Day" Virgin Express spaceship.

NO ONE CLIMBS EVEREST

BRITISH MOUNTAINEERS CELEBRATE CORONATION BY STAYING AT HOME

As dawn broke over the Himalayas, an astonishing scene greeted the world's media. For the first time in living memory, no one climbed Everest for an entire day.

Said veteran guide Sherpa Howard, "It was eerie. The great peak towering above us, with not a single climber in sight."

The timing could not have been more perfect. As the new king was crowned 10,000 miles away, not a single British person could be seen standing on the summit of the world's highest mountain, waving a Union Jack and throwing away an empty lager can.

A Coronation Text Message from the Computer Laureate

WL DN CHZ U R KING GR8! ☺

POOH BRICKS

bob. after EHS

CHURCH OF ENGLAND TO ACCEPT HETEROSEXUALS

by Our Religious Affairs Staff **Phil Pews**

THE Archbishop of Canterbury, Dr Rowan Williams, faced fierce opposition from traditionalists when he announced yesterday that he would bless "heterosexual marriages".

The Straight and Narrow-minded

A furious Bishop of Bath and Sauna said, "He is throwing away centuries of the church's history by pandering to a tiny minority of so-called 'straights'."

The Archbishop, however, was unrepentant. "We have to face the fact that in the twenty-first century there are a few people who are not homosexual and enjoy fulfilling relationships with members of the opposite sex." He continued, "We have to embrace them even if the thought of it is frankly rather unpleasant."

Dr Rowan Atkinson is currently appearing in the hit comedy film 'Mr Beard'.

NEW-LOOK QUEEN Pt. 94

You had the right idea, girl. No bloody kids!

GOVERNMENT'S NEW PLANS FOR SCHOOLS

by Our Education Staff **Phail Space**

THE EDUCATION Secretary, Mr Fungus Bogeyman, has revealed the Government's new strategy for "putting the fun back into education".

Mr Bogeyman told reporters that "children are under too much pressure from targets and tests".

"What I am doing is to make education more enjoyable by underfunding schools so that they have to close down and send pupils home."

Fungus and Games

He continued: "So instead of boring old double maths and the literacy hour, the kids can have fun

Mr Charles Clarke

watching television at home."

Said Mr Bogeyman, "We want to teach children a lesson they will never forget – i.e. don't trust me, I'm a Bogeyman."

CRACKDOWN ON NHS 'TARGETS'

by Our Political Staff **Doctor Spin**

ADMITTING that the health service is collapsing because of the obsession with targets, Health Secretary Alan Millstone yesterday promised to cut targets by 50 percent before 2005.

"If we have reached our target," he said, "we can look forward to a 75 percent improvement in waiting list times by 2006. If we fail to meet the target, I can guarantee that people will only have to wait for three months before another crackdown is announced.

"I am now going to lie down, if I can find a bed."

Late News

The Health Secretary, Mr Alan Heartburn, also announced that the NHS will no longer be treating fat people, people who smoke, people who drink alcohol or people who get ill.

Andrew Motion's Crap Poem (*surely "Rap", Ed*) to Celebrate the 21st Birthday of Prince William

He da Man
Who gonna be king
Respec Brova,
And all dat sort of ting.

Snoop Doggy Motion,
Poet Laureate

P.S. Can me stay on in dis job when you is da boss man?

SHY WILLIAM UNHAPPY ABOUT STAMP ROLE

I don't want anyone to lick my backside

Your Royal Highness, on the occasion of your 21st birthday, thank you so much for taking time out of your busy schedule to answer our spoon questionnaire. May I first ask you, sire, whether you have a favourite spoon?

The Press are always trying to link me to one particular spoon, but at the moment I like all sorts of spoons...

But, sire, if I may press a point, are there special Royal spoons with crests and so forth that you can use?

I'm aware that there are traditional occasions when those spoons are part of the ritual and fabric of Royalty and obviously it will be my duty to employ them, but as of now I prefer to use the same spoons as everyone else.

What about at College, sire, at the ancient University of St Andrew's?

We all mucked in, nobody had their own private spoons, we all used each other's, you know, um...

I should imagine there were spoon high jinks were there not, sire?

Well, yes, some of my fellow undergraduates did, on occasion, throw a few spoons about during Rag Week, but not nearly as much as the Press made out.

I'm sorry to have to ask this, sire, but our readers would like to know about the reports that you were born with a spoon in your mouth, you know, a silver one...?

I'm afraid I'm not really at liberty to talk about that.

I'm sorry, sire. In that case, is there anything else you would like to share with us?

I'd just like to say that Her Majesty the Queen has done a magnificent job in cataloguing the Royal Spoon Collection, including the famous Leonardo Sweetex, which is a spoon specially designed to dispense lumps of sugar by a spring mechanism, which is pretty amazing really...

I am indebted to Your Majesty and I would not dream of asking you if anything amusing had ever happened to you in connection with a spoon.

Well, actually there was that time when Wombat and Rupert got hold of this spoon and shoved it...

Royal Press Officer: That's all we've got time for, Your Majesty.

NEXT WEEK: Estelle Morris – *"Me and My Morris."*

"It's a beacon school"

Nursery Times

30 May 2003

TARTS RETURNED TO KNAVE OF HEARTS

BY OUR COURT STAFF ROB ROYALS

The Knave of Hearts removing the tarts for 'safe-keeping'

THE controversial Royal Knave, Mr Paul Butler, said last night that he was "delighted" to be given back his cherished tarts which were, he said, "gifts" from the late Queen of Hearts.

Police had arrived at Mr Butler's home in a carriage filled with tarts which had been in their custody for the duration of the case of the *Knave vs. Regina Cordarum*.

Mr Butler told the Daily Mirror Mirror On The Wall that "The Queen of Hearts always said that if anything happened to her, I was to take the tarts and hide them under my bed." He continued, "That is how the baked items that the police discovered came to be in my possession."

The Knave of Hearts went on to criticise the police for their "violation of his rights" in removing the tarts.

"It ruined my summer's day," he said, "and *(cont. p. 94)*

(cont. p. 94)

TOMORROW EXCLUSIVE

'The late Queen of Hearts – was she murdered?' asks the Knave, in the hope of getting in the paper again.

ARMY STRUGGLE WITH RECONSTRUCTION WORK

BY RADIO 4's AWARD-WINNING JOHN HUMPTYS

A SPOKESMAN for all the King's horses and all the King's men defended the role of the military as they tackled the difficult task of reconstructing Humpty Dumpty.

"This isn't strictly our job," said General Armchair. "The role of the modern army is to seek out and destroy unstable eggs. Cleaning up the mess afterwards is something for which we have not been trained."

He concluded, "Local militias on the ground are in a better position to return Humpty Dumpty to normal than we are."

LATE NEWS

Grand Old Duke Of York arrested for war crimes – did he march men to the top of the hill and then pistol whip them down again?

SUMMER CATALOGUE FROM *GNODENS*

THE *Sandringham* RANGE

William is wearing an Indian cotton long-sleeved Hooray shirt with blue denim stone-washed Sloane jeans. His boxer shorts (not shown) are from the Charles Moore Collection. Size: Small, Medium, Large house in the country. All items £6,000 (plus p&p). **William is 21 and an heir to the throne, living in St Andrews. His favourite soup is Brown Windsor. Ambition: To be King.**

"I hate 'reality' TV – bring back the Christians and lions"

Do you see a case for spoons?

In principle I am in favour of the spoon as a common-sense solution to the stirring problem. But I am not saying it is the *only* solution and I am not convinced that alternative stirring implements are not equally viable.

What are the alternatives?

Well, experience has shown that the plastic or wooden stirrer may be just as effective in the short term without the expense and complication of the spoon option.

But you are not ruling out spoons at some future date?

Let me make this clear. My position on spoons has always been consistent. I am in favour of spoons but only if the advantages of spoon use have been demonstrated to my satisfaction. Obviously a spoon would be very useful for picking up peas but the fact remains that we in this country have always used a fork for that purpose. Should we abandon this pragmatic and traditional approach merely to appease the supporters of the spoon?

You're sounding very spoon-sceptic.

Not at all. If you examine what I've just said I think you'll find I am very supportive of the spoon. It is all a matter of timing. When we should use a spoon and when we should stick to a fork or knife. This is not an all or nothing decision. I have to be satisfied that the conditions are right for the spoon and then – and only then – will I embrace it as the best way forward.

Has anything amusing ever happened to you in connection with a spoon?

This is not a subject that lends itself to humour, in my view.

NEXT WEEK: Andrew Motion – "Me and My Motions."

BLAIR TO PRODUCE NEW DOSSIER

by Our Economics Staff **Sterling Loss**

THE Prime Minister today publishes a 3,000-page dossier on the evidence for joining the Euro.

In it he claims that Britain is only 45 minutes away from economic disaster if we do not abolish the evil pound at once.

M.I. Sixpence

The Prime Minister quoted intelligence sources which made it absolutely clear that these pounds were capable of destroying the entire British economy and could destabilise the entire Euro-region unless they were "taken out" and a "currency change" implemented as soon as possible.

M.I. Fiver

"Future generations would not forgive us," he said, "if we sat on our hands and did nothing."

He continued, "Britain will be welcomed with open arms by grateful Europeans who will be delighted to see the end of the hated pound."

On other pages

Aerial photograph showing secret factory producing lethal coins (Royal Mint) **94**

COUGH BREAKS SILENCE

by Our Political Staff **Meg O'Zone**

THE LEADER of the Conservative Party, Mr Iain Duncan Cough, last night stunned the political world by breaking his self-imposed 12-month silence on the vexed question of British entry into the euro.

In front of hundreds of reporters, at a specially summoned Central Office press conference, Mr Cough strode to the microphone and issued his long-awaited statement.

"Ahem!" he began. As the waiting newsmen craned forward to hear what was to come next, the leader of the opposition placed his hand to his mouth and emitted the unmistakable sound of a faint cough.

At this, the Tory statesman turned decisively on his heel and exited the podium, leaving it to his shadow spokesman Mr Oliver Lctslose to unravel the deeper significance of Mr Cough's historic statement.

Don't Be Vague, Bring Back Hague

"What I think Iain is trying to say, and to my mind has said very eloquently, is that, if the government wants to have a national debate on the euro, then let's have it, by all means.

"It's not that we're mad Little Englanders who are bonkers about bent bananas or anything, it's just that we in the Tory Party do think that the euro is a tremendously important issue, and that, as Iain has so forcibly said in his statement today, it's time the British people were really given a chance to hear the arguments, both for and against, as Iain has so rightly pointed out, and that is why *(cont'd p. 94)*

GLENDA SLAGG

FLEET STREET'S WEAPON OF MAN DESTRUCTION!!!

■ HILLARY CLINTON – What a star!!? She's America's First Lady when it comes to Standin' By Your Man!?!! Good on you, babe!!?! Your two-timing hubby may have thought he'd got away with it, but now he's paying the Bill!!??! Now *you're* the one who's making millions and making it to the White House!!!!? You get my vote any day?!?

■ HILLARY CLINTON – What a two-timing cow!?!?! America's First Lady???!? You must be joking!!?!? America's First Bitch more like??!? Fancy dishing the dirt on poor old Bill when all he did was have a bit of fun with busty Monica!!?!?! Who wouldn't???!? Particularly if the option was dried up old stick Hillary!!?!? Take your rotten old memoirs, dearie, and jump off Brooklyn Bridge!!?!?!

■ *NANCY DELL'OLIO!!!!?!?? What a star??!??? She's Britain's First Lady when it comes to Standin' By Your Man??!!!? Good on you, babe!!??!!?* (Haven't we had this bit? Ed.)

■ NANCY DELL'OLIO!!!? What a two-timing cow!!?!?! (You've done this. Ed.)

■ HERE THEY ARE – Glenda's Barbecue Boys!!!

● **Alan Yentob** – *Imagine* giving yourself a job on the telly???!? Geddit???! Great beard, cute arts (geddit????!) Botney-baby!!!!??

● **Alastair Campbell** – You can sex me up any day of the week, Big Boy??? Geddit??!?!?

● **Kriskin** – Crazy name, crazy horse??!?

Byeeee!!!

POETRY CORNER

In Memoriam James Coburn, film actor

So. Farewell
Then James
Coburn.

Yes, we remember
You – the thin
One who threw
The knives in
*The Magnificent
Seven.*

What a great film.
And what a
Theme tune.

Dum. Di-da-da-dum.
Dum. Di-da-da-dum.

Then

Da-da
Di-da-DA-da.

Unfortunately I do not
Have the space
To reproduce
The entire
Score.

> E. J. Thribb
> (The Magnificent
> Seventeen-and-a-half)

In Memoriam Connex South East

So. Farewell
Then
Connex South East.

You have been
Sacked.

"We apologise for
The late running of
The 7.19."
That was your catchphrase.

"We apologise for
The cancellation of
The 7.19."
That was another.

Now you really are
'The late
Train service'.

> E.J. Thribb
> (17½ minutes late)

Scenes You Seldom See

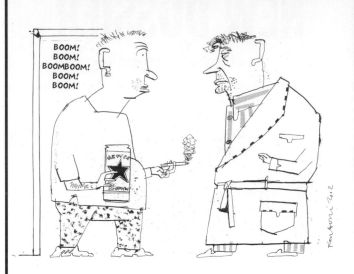

"Music too loud? Sorry, mate – I'll turn it down immediately"

"Oh, hi! Come on in. I've often thought about being a Jehovah's Witness"

"Hello, it's the builder. Just to let you know, we've finished the job on time and it will cost you three grand less than the estimate"

In Memoriam Brad Dexter, film star

So. Farewell
Then Brad
Dexter.

You were one of
The Magnificent Seven.

I am not quite sure
Which one
You were
But I think you died
Quite early on
In the big fight
At the end.

For the theme tune
I refer you to
My earlier poem
On the death of
James Coburn –
The one with
The knife.

Even so, it is difficult
Not to think of it
As I write.

Dum. Di-da-da-dum.
Dum. Di-da-da-dum.

Then

Da-da
Di-da-DA-da
(contd. p. 94)

> E. J. Thribb
> (The one with the poem)

In Memoriam Lonnie Donegan, singer of *Rock Island Line* and other hits

So. Farewell
Then Lonnie
Donegan,
King of
Skiffle.

Skiffle.
It is a strange
Word.

What does it
Mean?

Now you are
Gone
Perhaps we shall
Never know.

> E. J. Thribble (17½)

In Memoriam Sir Paul Getty, Philanthropist

So. Farewell then
Sir Paul Getty.

One of the world's
Richest men,
You were best known
For giving money to many
Good causes.

And to many artists,
Writers and
Poets.

But not
To me.

Despite my many letters
Suggesting it.

But I don't hold it
Against you.
You mean
Bastard!

    E. John-Paul Thribb
    (£17½ million would have
    been appreciated)

In Memoriam Horst Buchholz

So. Farewell then
Horst Buchholz.

You were in
The Magnificent Seven.
You were the young one
Who fell in love
With the beautiful Mexican
Girl at the end.

In recent months
We have said farewell to
James Coburn
And the other one, whose
Name no one
Can remember.

Yes, you are nearly
All gone.

But the music will live on.
Dum. Di-da-da-dum.
Dum. Di-da-da-dum.
Da-Da.
Di-da-DA-da.

    E.J. Thribb
    (The Magnificent
    Seventeen-and-a-half)

Scenes You Seldom See

"Normally we stop serving at 2 o'clock – but it's only five past, so what would you like?"

"Can you put me back on hold? I was really enjoying the music"

"You are clearly pregnant, my dear lady – have my seat"

In Memoriam Joan Littlewood, Theatre Impresario

So. Farewell
Then Joan
Littlewood.

With your
Famous cap
Set at a
Jaunty angle
On your head

You were the
Face of British
Theatre in the
Sixties.

Now the
Curtain has
Come down

And fings
Ain't wot
They used
To be.

    E. J. Thribb (17½)

In Memoriam Peter Bromley, racing commentator

So. Farewell then
Peter Bromley,
The BBC's
'Voice of racing'.

"Yes, it's Red Rum!
YES, IT'S RED RUM!
YES, IT'S RED RUM!"

That was your
Catchphrase.
Now you too have reached
The finishing post,
"Yes, it's Peter Bromley!"

    E.J. Thribb
    (17½ to 1)

Lines on the 100th Birthday of Bob Hope, Comedian

So. Not farewell then,
Yet.

    E.J. Thribb
    (117½)

Where's WMD?

YES, IT'S BACK! The puzzle sensation that will keep you occupied for months. Can YOU find the weapons of mass destruction hidden somewhere in Baghdad? No. That's because there aren't any. Now who's the Wally?

© T. Blair Publishing

WEAPONS INSPECTORS FIND 'THE SMOKING PANTS'

by W.M. Deedes

A TEAM of UN inspectors have at last reported the discovery of the vital evidence in the hunt for the Iraqi Weapons of Mass Destruction – a pair of smoking pants believed to have been worn by Tony Blair.

"If these pants are genuine," said Mr Hansup, "then it proves that they were definitely on fire whilst Blair was wearing them and that all his statements about WMDs were lies."

Mr Bliar is 50 (or maybe he isn't – you never know with him).

Tyrannosaurus Sex

HUNTer

BUSH SORTS MIDDLE EAST OUT

So, tell me again – which one of you is the Jewish guy?

ZIMBABWE – OUR BOYS DON'T GO IN

by Our War Staff
Sir Kevin Keegan and
Rageh Omaar Sharif

BRITAIN's greatest war-time prime minister of the 21st century today told the UN Security Council that Britain had no plans to force "regime change" on Zimbabwe.

"Mugabe," he said, "has shown the world that he is a murderous dictator who has subjected his own people to years of systematic torture and brutal repression.

"It would be all too easy to invade the country and topple this hated dictator, so that his people can be free.

"But I have to tell you, in all sincerity, that history would not forgive us if we acted now, rather than doing nothing.

"All morality dictates that we must stand idly by and let Mr Mugabe do whatever he likes."

Mr Blair later visited Aldershot where he addressed cheering troops, telling them "the country deeply appreciates your superb professionalism in keeping your barracks clean and polishing your boots, rather than going off to Africa to fight in some silly neo-colonialist war."

John Simpson reports from the BBC Canteen

There is an eerie calm here in London tonight as the whole nation prepares not to go to war.

Here in White City I can tell you that the mood is tense, as people face the moment of decision which will dictate whether they watch the snooker or Big Brother 7 (cont. p. 94)

'SARA COX INVADED MY PRIVACY' LISTENERS CLAIM
Huge Damages Sought

by Our Media Staff **D.J. Taylor**

THOUSANDS of listeners to Radio One claimed yesterday that the disc jockey Sara Cox had come into their front room and talked about sex with no prior consent on their part.

Said one typical listener, "I was disgusted. It was eight in the morning, I was just giving the kids breakfast and there she was polluting the air with her foul language, non-stop smut and sleazy innuendo."

Ms Cox, however, defended her actions, claiming that she had a perfect right to expose herself on radio since it was "a public place" and people had a perfect right to hear her being disgusting if they wanted to (cont. 94 MHz)

Lines Written on the Abolition of the Ancient Office of Lord Chancellor

By William Rees-McGonagall

'Twas in the year two thousand and three
That Prime Minister Tony Blair came out with a most
                                    astonishing decree.
With one stroke of the pen and a wave of his hand
He abolished the most ancient and important post in the
                                    land.

For centuries the office of Lord Chancellor had been
Second in importance only to that held by the King or
                                    Queen.
Many a famous man had held this rank in days of yore –
One thinks of Lord Hailsham and Sir Thomas More.

From the Woolsack the Chancellor presided over many a
                                    grand session
As speaker of the House of Lords, as well as head of the
                                    legal profession.
The appointment of judges was also in their power,
Even though some of those they promoted were an
                                    absolute shower.

Dressed up to the nines in their breeches and wig
Many thought that for their boots they had got too big,
Which brings me to the final holder of this post,
Whose pomposity and arrogance were accounted the most.

Lord Irvine of Lairg was this luminary's name,
Whose love of the bottle soon won him fame.
But nothing was to equal his taste in expensive wallpaper
E'en though it was the taxpayer who footed the bill for
                                    this caper.

Nor was this the only remarkable lapse in his private life
Since he had once run away with a trusted colleague's
                                    wife.
I have no wish at this stage to descend into the sewer,
But it may be recalled that this lady was Mrs Donald
                                    Dewar.

Lord Irvine owed his high position to his former pupil Tony.
Indeed many considered him to be the quintessential crony.
He considered that he had been given a job for life
Along with a huge pension for himself and his wife.

But he had not reckoned with the fickleness of his
                                    Master Blair
Whose fine words turned out as usual to be no more
                                    than hot air.
Like Beckett and More just as he'd reached the top
He was summoned to hear that he'd been given the chop.

And so, with the sacking of this one time friend,
Blair brought fourteen hundred years of history to an end.
A mighty shout of protest ran round the nation
At this shocking act of constitutional desecration.
Which was odd because when it was mentioned before
They had all agreed that Lord Irvine of Lairg was a
                                    thumping great bore.

Blair To Abolish 'Oldest Post In Land'

by Our Political Staff
Christopher Howseoflords

THE WORLD of Westminster was rocked to its foundations last night when Tony Blair announced through Sky News that he was planning to abolish the ancient and respected office of the Queen.

Her Majesty was said to be "livid" that she was not consulted about her own abolition.

Mr Blair is thinking of replacing her with his oldest friend – himself.

Those New Ministerial Posts In Full

- Secretary of State For Transport, Skills, Scotland and Fisheries **Alistair Prescott**
- Secretary of State for Constitutional Affairs, Leisure, the Media and Wales **Peter Straw**
- Secretary of State for Foreign Affairs, Health, the Regions and Airports **Estelle Reid**
- Secretary of State for Overseas Development, Women's Affairs, Sport and Defence **John Darling**
- Secretary of State for Lifelong Learning, Sustainability, Convergence, Transparency, Europe, Grapefruit Segments and Northern Ireland **Baroness Morris**

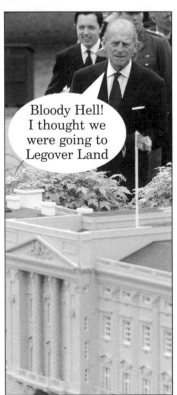

Bloody Hell! I thought we were going to Legover Land

ME AND MY SPOON

THIS WEEK

BORIS JOHNSON

Do you like spoons?

Cripes! I wasn't expecting that one! I need a bit of time to think about it. Spoons, eh? Yes, well, I wouldn't say no to a spoon. Jolly good chaps, spoons. Can't have enough of them!

So you wouldn't want any regulations on spoons?

Now, hang on. You're trying to trick me into saying something here, I know. Let's sort this out. No, I'm all in favour of people having as many spoons as they like. So long as they don't start chucking them at each other. I mean, that wouldn't be in anyone's interest, would it? Blimey! You're really putting me in the hot seat, aren't you?

Do you think Iain Duncan Smith is a spoon person?

Oh no, you won't catch me that easily! I saw that one coming. Lips sealed. No comment. Boris remains shtum. There's your headline, chum.

What do you think about all these Tories having affairs?

Jeepers creepers! What's that got to do with spoons? I thought that's what this interview was all about. You're trying to make me look an idiot, aren't you?

Has anything amusing ever happened to you in connection with a spoon?

No.

NEXT WEEK: The Dalai Lama – *"Me and My Llama"*.

BECKHAM KIDNAP CASE THROWN OUT OF COURT

by Our Legal Staff **Joshua Rosenberg**

THE BECKHAM kidnap trial collapsed yesterday when the judge ruled that the prosecution case was based on "an obvious hoax" viz that the News of the World was a newspaper.

The judge said, "It is quite evident that there has been a deliberate deception practised on all parties by a gang of unsavoury individuals masquerading as journalists."

News of the Screwups

He told the court, "This gang, led by a woman called Rebekah, was out to take as much money as it could from the public. One of the members, Mr Mazher Mahmood, posed as a reporter in order to persuade gullible readers to buy fabricated stories about Posh and Becks. He has a long history of doing this sort of thing, sometimes dressing up in full costume with a dirty raincoat and a trilby hat with a ticket marked 'Press' stuck in the brim."

Mazzive Fraud

In his defence, Mr Mahmood said, "It was perfectly legitimate for me to disguise myself as a journalist, otherwise people would have been suspicious when I gave them a huge cheque for making things up."

Dosh and Bucks

The judge, however, concluded that there was no evidence whatsoever that the News of the World was a newspaper or that it was ever going to run a legitimate story.

"The whole thing," he summed up, "is a sleazy, money-making scam."

The former editor of the News of the World, Ms Rebekah Wad, said that the judge's account of events was a tissue of lies and offered him £20,000 for the serialisation.

"Doesn't he look different on television?"

THE BIG READ

Britain's 100 Best-Loved Novels That Have Been Made Into Films

No. 94
Rebekah
by Daphne Du Moron

"LAST NIGHT I dreamed of Money again..." The unforgettable opening sentence of Britain's 94th best-loved romantic novel plunges us at once into the mysterious world of flame-haired tempestuous beauty Rebekah who has fallen under the spell of the evil but fabulously rich foreign financier Rupert le Digger.

What is his dark secret? Why is everyone in his employ obsessed with Money? Why does he keep looking at her in an odd way, as if he feels he has made a terrible mistake? What is the explanation for the mysterious telephone calls in the middle of the night? And what is the relationship between the ruthless billionaire and his sinister Oriental housekeeper Mrs Wendy Dengvers? Will the atmosphere of growing menace culminate in someone being fired?

GOVERNMENT BOWS TO REFERENDUM DEMAND

By our Political Staff **Simon Hefferendum**

THE WORLD of politics was shaken to its core when the Government announced that it would give the public a chance to vote on the most important constitutional issue of their lifetime.

Not the Euro

Said the Deputy Prime Minister, John Prescott, "Wherever I go people are talking about nothing else but the need for Regional Assemblies in the North of England. It's the single issue on everyone's mind and it is much more of a priority than schools, hospitals, transport or anything else."

Not True

Mr Prescott continued, "We are a listening government and what we are hearing is a constant barrage of demands for a new tier of local government.

"There is only one honest course of action open to us and that is to hold an immediate referendum on the pressing issue of avoiding talking about Europe." *(Surely 'restructuring autonomous regional administration to decentralize zzzzzzzzzzz'. Ed.)*

I would be very happy to enter the euro

BRITAIN FACES NEW TERROR WARNING

by Our Man In The Bunker **Al Corena**

BRITAIN braced itself yesterday for a possible MI5 warning that could be delivered "at any minute".

Said the Head of MI5 Elizabeth Bullying-Manner "There is a group of dedicated professionals who are determined to spread terror throughout the country. These MI5 operatives could strike at any minute, possibly in the Daily Telegraph or almost certainly in the Daily Mail with a warning that Dirty Bombs may lead to a fall in house prices."

She continued, "The public must all be vigilant and tell us what is going on because we don't have a clue."

"We'll bung you a few grand if you take out the anti-corruption clauses"

E.U. CONSTITUTION

Seamus Heaney's 'Beowulf'

as translated by Eminem

Big fucking monster givin
everyone shit

Along comes Beowulf and he
ain't taking it

Kills the motherfucker
Grendel with a big fucking
sword

Then kills the motherfucker's
mother cos he's so fucking
bored.

Writes Seamus Heaney: In this wonderfully energetic recreation of the 8th Century masterpiece, Mr Eminem conveys a sense of spiritual and poetic discovery that we have not known since the work of Bob Dylan and John Lennon. I don't want to "diss" more conventional poetry, but we must admire (cont. p. 94)

The Alternative Rocky Horror Service Book

No. 94 A Service for the Enthronement of a Celibate Gay Bishop

President *(for it is she)***:** Brethren and sisters of all genders and orientations, we are gathered here for the solemn induction of our brother _____ into the bishopric of _____ in the diocese of _____ .

Before we can proceed to the ceremony you are required to answer certain questions in the presence of Almighty God and the assembled media.

Q: Do you solemnly admit that you are totally gay?

A: Indeedy, I do.

Q: And are you proud to be gay?

A. I am proud so to be.

Q: Are you in a long-established and stable relationship with your live-in same sex partner?

A. Yes, _____ and I have been in a state of co-habitation for_____ years.

Q: Are you now entirely celibate; with no physical union, one with another, in the eyes of the Lord?

A. Can I phone a friend?

Q: Do you undertake to remain in a state of Holy celibacy for as long as ye both shall live?

A. I will do my best with regard to that one.

President: I now pronounce you Bishop and celibate partner. Whom God hath joined together, may no tiresome woman set asunder.

HYMN

"The gay though gavest, Lord, is now the bishop"

THE BLESSING

New Bishop: Bless!

The congregation shall then process out to the accompaniment of Jeremiah Clarke's Trumpet Voluntary Celibacy *(no organ please!)*.

COUGH SPLUTTERS AT POLL SHOCK

by Our Political Staff **Benny Lyn**

THE world of politics was rocked to its foundations last night by a new poll showing that the Conservative Party had recorded a 2-point lead over Labour for the first time in a decade.

All over Westminster MPs were fainting in disbelief at the news, none more so than Mr Duncan Cough, the Tory leader, who was said by aides to be "speechless".

"This was not at all what we were expecting," said one of Cough's closest allies. "All our own surveys have shown that 95 percent of the electorate believe the Tory party is totally useless, and that Iain is the worst party leader in the history of the world.

"We therefore discount this rogue poll as merely a mid-term blip and we are confident that the overall trend will soon continue its downward course."

ART

Brian Sewell at The Royal Academy Summer Exhibition

What A Load Of Vulgar Old Tat!

FOR over half a century I have each year viewed with infinite distaste the talentless squaubs and daubs that are passed off to the long-suffering British public as "art", run up by super-annuated schoolmistresses in their bed-sits in Woking, who think that a flatulent water-colour imitation of some package-holiday souvenir postcard showing La Serenissima by moon-light with a mangy cat sitting in the foreground is somehow worthy to be considered as standing in the tradition of Canaletto and Turner (or even Sickert in his pre-Camden Town heyday), and every year I write the same piece.

© R. Sewell 1953-2003.

"What are you like at filing?"

"I'll give it a go"

BABY TO GIVE BIRTH TO OWN MOTHER

by Our Medical Staff **M. Brio**

IN AN astonishing breakthrough for medical science, researchers at the Bram Stoker Institute for Human Development in New Zombie, California have developed a new technique whereby the frozen eggs of aborted foetuses can be implanted into the transplanted womb of a same-sex partner and fertilised by the frozen sperm of a dead gay bishop, thus producing an embryo which can then be genetically modified to become a large tomato.

Dr Frank N. Stein

Which Came First, The Money Or The Egg?

Said the head of the clinic, Dr Frank N. Stein, "We are very excited by this development, which will allow a lot of childless couples to enjoy the richly fulfilling experience of becoming their own salad". *(Surely "mothers"?)*

His partner Dr Acula added, "We are now like proud parents, looking forward to the safe delivery of a large and healthy cheque."

Last night a spokesman for The Human Embryological Ethics And In Vitro Fertilisation Authority said that there was no evidence that eating eggs could cause BSE but "under the precautionary principle we recommend that all fish should be destroyed six weeks before birth".

CHARLES IN GM STORM

By our Political Staff **GMT Vee**

THE PRINCE of Wales last night launched an astonishing personal attack on science minister Lord Sainsbury, warning him to "Keep out of politics".

Lord Sainsbury has for some time been a passionate advocate of non-organic food, and has issued apocalyptic warnings of the dangers to mankind of not growing genetically modified crops.

But Prince Charles has had enough of the interfering supermarket chief. "He is an unelected hereditary millionaire," said the Prince, "who has only got his position because of who his family is.

Off His Trolley

"He should stick to his job, going round the country talking to check-out girls and opening new supermarkets.

"He should leave politics to people who know what they're talking about, like me," said the Prince.

Daily Mail, Friday, June 27, 2003

Nigel Dumpster's Diary

Top Diarist's Day of Shame

■ I HAVE SAD news for myself, 62, following my unfortunate appearance yesterday before Old Etonian judge Mr Justice Cocklecarrot, 72, brother of the better-known bon viveur and motor racing enthusiast *(get on with the case – ED).*

Finding the Sherborne-educated myself guilty of drunk driving, the elderly but still sprightly judge joked that he had never come across such a flagrant and disgraceful liar in all his 42 years on the bench.

Quick as a flash, the sharp-witted and elegantly-dressed myself, immaculately clad in a pinstripe blue suit with a silver and purple old Shirburnian tie, quipped back, 'Of course I'm a liar, your honour, I write a gossip column in the Daily Mail.'

The judge, I am glad to say, looked suitably abashed as he sentenced me to ten years' hard labour.

Duke's Daughter Unconcerned

■ I AM sorry to hear that Lady Camilla Dumpster, seventh daughter of the 89th Duke of Maidstone and a distant kinswoman by marriage of Her Late Majesty, Queen Elizabeth the Queen Mother, 106, has expressed, 'total indifference' to the tragic fate of her estranged husband, myself, who was yesterday sentenced to 50 years of penal servitude in Botany Bay, following a misunderstanding over a drunken driving incident.

When I rang her yesterday to pass on the sad tidings, she told me, 'I am sorry, there is no one here to take your call at present, but if you would like to leave a message I will get back to you, unless you are my husband, in which case you can get stuffed.'

Lady Camilla was last night said to be not being comforted by friends.

Lady Camilla is 61.

Piss-Ed!

■ TOP EDITOR Paul Dacre, 72, whose son Kevin, 17, is at school at Eton with Prince William, 21, and Prince Harry, 18, is said by close friends to be 'furious' with his diarist, myself, following an astonishing personal attack by a judge, who accused the balding but debonair man-about-town, myself, of 'shamelessly lying' to cover up his serial offences as a drunken driver.

Sources close to Dacre told me exclusively yesterday: 'Paul has put up with your piss-poor column for years, but this could well be the last straw.' Is this the end for myself, colleagues were asking last night as they toasted the judge in champagne.

Gossip Man – Mystery Grows

■ FRIENDS of myself were asking last night whether I was still writing this column, following my conviction and sentencing to death for drunken driving earlier this week.

The answer is of course, 'No, of course not, it's being written by some Sloaney girls, just like it always has been, while I am driving around town pissed.'

Old Rhymes Revisited

Humpty Dumpster crashed into a wall
Humpty Dumpster said he hadn't drunk anything
at all.

All the Queen's counsel and all the top men,
Couldn't stop Humpty from being banned from ever
driving again.

© All papers except the Daily Mail.

HARRY POTTER PUBLISHED AMIDST SCENES OF PANDEMONIUM

By our Literary Staff **Simon Hogwarts**

THE NEW Harry Potter book was published at midnight last night to the delight of thousands of journalists who had queued up all night to get their articles into the paper.

Many of the journalists had been waiting for months and their joy at the launch of the book was uncontained. Said one young enthusiast Peter Thomson, 14, "It's just fantastic. It's a terrific story and I can't wait to write it up."

Some critics have worried that the Harry Potter story has been going on too long but this opinion is not shared by the diehard fans in the press.

"We can't get enough of Harry", said a beaming Charles Moore, 11½, "He's wonderful and has the magic power to fill up our paper without us having to put any news in."

PAXMAN UNDER MAGIC SPELL SHOCK

So will you answer any of my questions?

No

That's fine by me. I won't press you

The children of the Eye's staff give their verdict of the new Harry Potter novel

Tina Slagg, 12
Harry Potter donchaluvhim? Harry Potter arenchasickofhim?

Quentin Spart, 8
Basically a sickening endorsement of public school privilege which is utterly and totally nauseating… er… I loved it.

Emma Thribb, 17½ months
So Farewell Then
All my other books.

Charlie Filler, 3
Not nearly as good as my mother's book, *Mummy for Old Rope,* available in all good bookshops (signed in his absence by P. Filler).

TOP 10 BESTSELLERS

(As supplied by Tesco, Britain's leading bookseller)

1. Harry Potter And The Weapons Of Mass Destruction
2. Harry Potter And The Dodgy Dossier
3. Harry Potter And The 23 Shirt
4. Harry Potter And The Gay Bishop
5. Harry Potter And The Bridget Riley Exhibition
6. Harry Potter And The Reform Of The Common Agricultural Policy
7. Harry Potter And The Bin Laden Lookalike

(That's enough Harry Potter books. Ed.)

WIMBLEDON

Sex to Watch

(Surely 'Six to Watch'? Ed)

The *Eye*'s Guide to the Top Women Players

Krikey Donchaluva, 21, new blonde bombshell from the Lezch Republic. With her long legs and blonde hair, Krikey is set to go all the way to Page 3

Tina Lollita, 17, the Number One from Nabokovia is the clear favourite of the middle-aged sports editor and this may be her year to lose her temper with the photographers

Butchia Dykova, 33, is Lesbia's top-ranking player who is set to win the hearts of no-one at all with her powerful serve, strong groundstrokes and general ability to play tennis

Britt Hopeless, 38, is the homegrown darling of the Centre Court who will go down in history as well as the first round if she keeps up her current run of bad form

Anna Rexia, 5 ½ stone, the young challenger from Bulimia looks like going all the way to the Wimbledon hospital to be treated for an eating disorder

Somebody Williams, 26, the American-born winner will win as usual *(That's enough, Ed)*

THE LAWN TENNIS ASSOCIATION

IN

YOU FXXXING WXXKER

OUT

77

The Alternative Rocky Horror Service Book

No. 95 A Service for the Standing Down of an Appointee Gay Bishop

President (The Archbishop of Canterbury, for it is he): Brothers and Brothers we are gathered together here today in a spirit of great sadness to lament the standing down of our brother _____ and his live-in celibate partner _____ who has, let's face it, also been sharing the terrible traumas of the past few weeks.

(The congregation shall all make the "Sign of Disapproval". They may tut or shake their heads or make some such gesture indicating sympathy with the non-appointee.)

President: Who giveth away his job?

Non-Appointee: I do.

President: Do you promise to go quietly and not to give interviews to the media?

Non-Appointee: I so promise.

President: I now declare you Non-Bishop of Reading.

(The evangelical members of the congrega-tion may now hug each in exultation.)

Evangelicals: Hallelujah!

CONFESSION

President: We shall now confess our faults before God, particularly the Bishop of Oxford whose stupid idea this whole thing was in the first place.

Bishop of Oxford: Good morning, Brian. Good morning, Sarah. You know, in a very real sense it wasn't my fault at all. It was the Archbishop of Canterbury's and I think we should all think about that as we move towards a more inclusive and gay-friendly Church of England.

READING

(There follows a reading by the Reverend Gay Friendly First Woman Bishop of Nova Scotia, taken from the Epistle to the Guardian.)

Reader: At the beginning of the twenty-first century it is frankly appalling that the Church should continue to discriminate against homosexuals. Didn't Our Lord himself never marry and consort with sailors around the Sea of Gallilee?

THE INTERRUPTION

(Here members of the African Churches may voice their disapproval.)

Bishop O'Nanugu Suffragan Bishop of Rumbabwe: I am not sittin' here listenin' to dis filth about sodomy and de liftin' of cassocks, but on de other hand, I give thanks to de Lord dat de Bishop of Reading is cast down into de fiery furnace wid all de other dirty buggers... Amen.

THE OFFERTORY

The Hymn *The Gay Thou Gavest Lord Has Ended* shall be sung whilst the offertory plate is passed around. The Evangelicals will keep their hands in their pockets, leaving the collection very small indeed.

THE DISMISSAL

President: You're fired. Get out.

Non-Appointee: *(Sob)*

All: This is a sad day for all of us *(or they may say "This is a glad day for all of us").*

RECESSIONAL HYMN

It's Raining Amen by The Weather Girls.

IN THE COURTS

Lady Archole v. Jane Gaffblower Day 94

Before Mr Justice Cocklecarrot

Sir Rumpole de Mellor QC *(representing Lady Archole):* My Lord, I represent one of the most distinguished scientists of our generation, the Lady Archole of Granchester, who is seeking an ex parte writ of *silenciamus* against the defendant, Ms Beanspiller, who used her position as private assistant to Lord Archole, one of the most distinguished *litterateurs* of this or any other age...

Cocklecarrot: Get on with it, Sir Rumpole, there is a very important tennis match I have to attend to.

Sir Rumpole: I am indebted to you. I would like to call my client, the Lady Archole, as my first witness. My Lady, you do, do you not, abhor the attentions of the media whatsoever they may be?

Lady Fragrantia Archole: Indeed, Sir Rumpole. Like my poor, dear late husband, Sir Toad of Toad Hall, so cruelly incarcerated in the deepest dungeon of the stoutest castle in all England for no more than the trifling offence of driving his bicycle without a light...

Cocklecarrot: Dear lady, I submit that you mean a most heinous act of perjury...

Lady Archole: Be that as it may, My Lord, you must know that so deep is my detestation of publicity of any kind, as I have made clear in countless newspaper interviews, that I have brought this case in a last-ditch attempt to keep my name and my private life out of the newspapers. The very last thing I would wish is to see the details of my recent face lift blazoned across the pages of every tabloid gossip sheet in the nation...

(Hacks rush from courtroom to file 'Lady Archole Admits To Face Lift Shock' stories to every tabloid gossip sheet in the land.)

The case continues...

LADY ARCHER SHOCK

I had a face lift

On which one?

BLAIR DEFENDS WAR ON BBC

by Our Defence Staff W.M. Deedes

THE PRIME Minister last night furiously defended his decision to launch an all-out attack on the BBC. He produced a special dossier compiled by top level intelligence officers (*Alastair Campbell*) which gives intricate details of the threat posed to Great Britain by the evil regime of Greg Dyke.

Aerial photographs show that the BBC has newsrooms all over the country which can launch devastating bulletins aimed at the Prime Minister "within 45 minutes".

Weapons of mass communication

The Prime Minister said, "Future generations will not forgive us if we do not seize this opportunity to destroy the BBC for good."

Greg "Saddam" Dyke is 58.

BBC bias row latest

The BBC is biased against us

The BBC is biased against us

We demand equal bias against us

HETEROSEXUAL JUDGE APPOINTED

BRITAIN's first heterosexual judge was appointed last night amidst claims that he would be unable to relate to the majority of the population (cont. p. 94)

GALLOWAY – SEARCH FOR WRIT GOES ON

by Our Special Correspondent **Christopher Silvester**

THE SEARCH for the elusive WMD, Writ for Massive Damages, goes on, despite weeks in which there has been no sign whatever of the writ.

The deadly writ, which was said to be only 45 minutes away from destroying the Daily Telegraph, has hitherto failed to materialise, but top WMD expert George Galloway refused to back down.

"I am absolutely confident," he said, "that the writ will be found and will justify my going into Iraq."

"If, at the end of the day, you can't have fun, what's the point?"

"That unless we hear from Mr Alastair Campbell by 11 o'clock this morning we will be in a state of war…"

AN APOLOGY FROM MRS HEWITT

Secretary of State for Trade and Industry

IN RECENT years, we as a government may have given the impression that the most important quality of a successful country was youthfulness. When the prime minister told the Labour Party Conference in 1997, 1998, 1999 and 2000 that he was proud to be the "young leader of a young country with young ideas and young energy taking Britain into a young future," the audience may have interpreted this as suggesting that Mr Blair believed youth was in some way a good thing.

We now realise, after looking at the shortfall in pension provision, that nothing is more important to the future of Britain than that old people should carry on making their immensely valuable contribution to society until they drop dead. Otherwise, without the inestimable benefits which flow from decades of experience and wisdom, the country is going to be completely bankrupt by 2015. On these grounds, the prime minister's theme at this year's party conference will be how proud he is to be an "old leader of an ancient country with its well-tried ideas and senile energy taking Britain into a historic future". We apologise for any confusion that may have been caused by these two apparently contradictory viewpoints.

PRINCE HARRY COMES OF AGE

So, how long have you been a piece of toast?

About three minutes, sir

PAPERS 'BACK ON THE BEST'

by Our Media Staff **Mutt and Jeff Bernard**

AFTER several months of abstinence, Britain's newspapers have fallen off the wagon in a spectacular orgy of articles about George Best.

For years it has been known that newspapers had a serious "Best problem". They couldn't get enough of him, day after day running huge articles about him being drunk.

At one time the Best addiction got so bad it looked as though it might kill off any interest in newspapers for ever.

But then, a year ago, came the heartening news that the papers had kicked the Best habit for good.

For weeks they didn't touch him at all, preferring a sober diet of harmless stories about David Beckham.

But yesterday it all went horribly wrong. As Best raised a glass to his lips, millions of hacks gave in to temptation and went on a three-day binge, writing article after article until they were all under the table with exhaustion.

On Other Pages

- ● I was an alcoholic 2
- ● So was I 3
- ● My wife was 3
- ● My husband is 4

Plus Dr Raj Perfraud, Dr James Le Foney and Dr Thomas Utterfraud on "What Happens When You Get Drunk".

BBC Radio 3

Opera on 3

Der Italianische Schweinhund
Gerhard Schroeder (1802-1861)
Opera in Three Acts

Act 1
The villain Berlusconi, an Italian robber chieftain, enters a wood near Brussels disguised as the prime minister of Italy. He points at a harmless German woodcutter, Schultz, and sings the aria *Du Bist Ein Nazi Kommandant*.

Act 2
There has been a revolution. Berlusconi is universally vilified and the patriotic citizens of Germany all refuse to go on holiday in Italy. They sing the famous Sunlounger Chorus *Wirfahren Nicht*.

Act 3
An unrepentant Berlusconi, now disguised as the President of the EU, accuses the German tourists of being fat, lager-drinking pigs in the cavatina *Die Grosse Schweinen von Deutschland*. War is declared between the two nations, and the opera comes to an abrupt end.

The Strasbourg Opera Chorus and Orchestra are conducted by Romano Prodi. The part of Windbaggio, the comic policeman, is sung by the Welsh tenor Neil Kinnock.

'Totalische und Utterlische'

ARCHER IS OUT

NANCY ANNOUNCES ENGAGEMENT

Sven has got a date in mind

Yes, but it's not you

Man Found With Work On Computer

by Our Internet Staff **P.D. File**

THE AUTHORITIES were warned of the growing "misuse" of computers by men who are using the internet to access "work-related" sites.

"This is not what computers are for," said a spokesman for the industry. "It is shocking, but we believe it is only a very small minority of men who are using their computers in this way."

Apple Dirty Mac

This follows the discovery of an unnamed man who was caught in his office writing an email to a work colleague. The man claimed that it was the first time he had ever done such a thing and he was merely doing it "out of curiosity".

The Internut

The 37-year-old recipient of the email was, however, "appalled" by the content of the communication which made graphic references to "outstanding invoices" and "unissued receipts".

Said the industry spokesman, "This is an abuse of the proper function of information technology, which is designed to facilitate the downloading of pornography and the attempted abduction of minors via chatrooms."

JEWISH COMEDIAN FLIES IN

by Our Man In The Front Stalls Of The Royal Opera House, **Jack E. Mason**

THE JEWISH comedian who has been hailed as the world's funniest man took centre stage in London last night and had audiences weeping uncontrollably with his own brand of tear gas.

Ariel Sharon has lost none of his old flair for slaying them in the aisles, as he showed when he quipped, "You want a settlement? I'll build you hundreds of them!"

And there was more. "Every time I tell that joke," he went on, "I bring the house down. Pity it had so many people still inside it!"

Even though the audience had heard this routine many times before, they nevertheless gave him a standing ovation, leaping to their feet and pleading with him not to shoot.

Jackie Mason is 103.

How Low Can You Stoop?

JAMES HEWITT's decision to broadcast the contents of letters from the late Princess Diana must rank as the most sordid act of betrayal in the history of treachery.

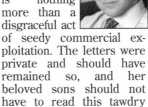

His squalid cashing-in on his sexual relationship with the late Princess of Wales under the guise of "historical record" is nothing more than a disgraceful act of seedy commercial exploitation. The letters were private and should have remained so, and her beloved sons should not have to read this tawdry filth.

On Other Pages

● Those Dirty Di Letters in full **2,3,4**
● How Good was Di In Bed? **5**
● Is Harry Hewitt's Love Child? **6**
● Simulated pix of Di and Hewitt at it **7, 8, 9, 10, 11**
● Unfunny Hewitt cartoon by Hac **69**

It's all in today's Special Soaraway Bumper Hewitt-Is-A-Bastard Souvenir Issue!!! Hurry, hurry, whilst shock lasts!

THIS WEEK

SIR MICHAEL CAINE

What do you remember about your childhood spoons?

You've got to be joking. We lived in a street where there was one spoon between ten families. My old Mum had to beg for the use of that spoon. The rest of the time we had to eat with our fingers – not that we had anything to eat. That's why all the snobs in this country try and put me down. I've had to work bloody hard to get the spoons I've got now and when you come back to this country after working in America the first thing that happens is that the taxman tries to take all your bloody spoons away. Take them away!

Did spoons feature prominently in "The Ipcress File"?

Some people in this country are born with bloody great silver spoons in their mouths. Lord this and Sir that but not me, my Dad worked in Billingsgate as a fish porter and…

Has anything amusing ever happened to you in connection with a spoon?

No. Not a lot of people know that.

NEXT WEEK: Anne Widdecombe – *"Me and My Comb."*

"Stand back – let it breathe!"

POETRY CORNER

In Memoriam Norman Panama, Hollywood scriptwriter

So. Farewell
Then Norman
Panama.

You wrote many
Unforgettable scripts
Such as *White Christmas*.

But best of all was
The Court Jester,
Starring Danny
Kaye.

The vessel with the pestle
Has the pellet with the poison
But the chalice from the palace
Has the brew that is true.

Yes. But later we found out
That the chalice from the palace
Was broken.
And the pellet with the poison
Was now in
The flagon with the dragon.

Or it might have been
The other way round.

Either way it was pure
Poetry.

> E. J. "The Doge" Thribb
> ('The Poet in the Paper with
> the Pen that is True')

In Memoriam Concorde

So. Farewell
Then,
Concorde.

Triumph of
Anglo-French
Technology.

You were
The fastest passenger
Plane ever
Built.

"Boom! Boom!"
That was your
Catchphrase.

"Bust! Bust!"
That is it
Now.

> E.J. Thribb (71½,000 mph)

82

SUPERMODELS

KERBER

GEOFFREY LEVY INVESTIGATES THE VIRGIN MARY

Over the years, the Virgin Mary has gone to desperate lengths to build up a reputation for simplicity and devotion – not to mention sexual purity.

Ordinary, decent, middle-class families the world over look up to her for her legendary care of the less-well-off. In some circles, her name has become a byword for charity. The Pope himself regards her as a saint.

But who, close friends are beginning to ask, is the REAL Virgin Mary?

Beneath her carefully-nurtured goody-two-shoes image, who is this woman with the floor-length robes who, friends say, has spent a lifetime battling with a multitude of weight problems?

Strutting the world in her costly designer cloaks – specially designed, experts maintain, to hide the way she see-saws between suffering from anorexia and letting herself go – the Virgin Mary has employed every trick in the book to foster her cleaner-than-clean public image.

To be fair, her earning power is undeniable. In the stark words of one former associate, she works hard and she plays hard. Yet key questions remain about this tactile career woman – questions that continue to baffle even her closest friends and former business associates.

And today these questions look set to rebound, possibly rocking her career and reputation to their very foundations.

So what drives the Virgin Mary?

Friends say that the real Mary is far removed from the saintly image. In fact, I can now reveal, she is a ruthless single parent career woman caught in a tragic love web.

Having grown up in a four-bedroomed luxury home set in two acres – valued at £250,000 in today's terms – the unmarried Mary stuck two fingers up at her hard-working parents by shouting her underage pregnancy from the rooftops.

HE was an ageing out-of-work labourer with no prospects to speak of.

SHE was an underage foreign girl with a baby on the way – and a burning desire to be famous.

Wearing an air of injured innocence – a mask which, former colleagues attest, she ruthlessly employs at all times – Mary managed to persuade the elderly Joseph to make an honest woman of her.

So who exactly was this Joseph – and how

could he have fallen for Mary's finely-honed manipulative skills?

Aided, no doubt, by the hard-pressed taxpayer, Joseph delighted in calling himself a carpenter. But – aside from tables and chairs and a full range of bedroom furniture – former friends are unable to recall anything he actually made. One even recalls a "slight tilt" to one of Joseph's much-vaunted tables.

So much for those earlier boasts of fine workmanship.

In truth, Joseph was a tragic old man who cut a pitiful figure in his rootless ethnic circles. But one thing was for sure. Joseph liked living well – event though, as close colleagues confirm, he had a fear of commitment. But, like many men before him, faced with a stunning young pregnant schoolgirl, this decrepit lothario found he just couldn't say no.

To this day, the Virgin Mary dines out on stories of THAT birth.

While many will find it hard to imagine any ordinary, decent mother wishing to regale her friends with tales of giving birth in a sordid cowshed, surrounded by salivating farmyard beasts, close investigation reveals that Mary is, in the words of one former colleague, "fixated with fame – even if it means turning a blind eye to basic hygiene".

Though there is as yet no firm evidence that Mary was at that time on hard drugs, former associates continue to voice their suspicions that the reason she seldom had time for drugs was that she was in the midst of her uphill struggle against weight problems. "If she'd had a mind to take drugs," says one close friend, "then, believe me, drugs are what she'd have taken."

The oddball couple soon made it clear that

they had, against the silent majority of concerned parents, decided to call the baby "Jesus".

"It's not a name I'd have chosen for a baby boy," says one former associate. "It makes me shudder to think of the teasing he got in school."

Incredible as it may seem to those who try to give their children a decent start in life, within minutes of the baby's birth Joseph and Mary allowed low-paid farm labourers into the stable to look at the baby.

It is not known whether the pair of them charged the labourers for this facility, but friends confirm that the unmarried couple made no secret of "often being short of a few bob". If the authorities later investigated the matter, their report has never come to light. Whether it was secretly destroyed on the say-so of Mary is a matter of speculation.

Next, it was the turn of the so-called "Three Kings", a shadowy, secretive sect of bachelors in flashy robes, at least one of them an unashamed representative of an ethnic minority. These three unsavoury characters brought small packages into the stable believed to contain "gold", "frankincense" and "myrrh". Recurrent rumours that they smuggled these substances into the stable intravenously have never been verified.

But one thing is clear. As one child expert puts it, "These are wholly unsuitable gifts for a new-born baby. This is a story that gives widespread cause for concern".

The tragedy of that tragic infant's life – tragic betrayal by a former associate, followed by tragic shame in the courts, and a tragic all-too-public death on the cross, topless – might have led other mothers to put the brakes on their tireless pursuit of headlines.

But not so the Virgin Mary.

Over the subsequent centuries, this ambitious daughter of hard-working parents has never turned up her nose at an opportunity for self-promotion, making ill-judged personal appearances in her signature halo at grottoes and shrines the world over. Perhaps, as friends suggest, it appeals to her massive ego.

She seems to have it all. Fame. Glamour. Friends in high places.

But will the Virgin Mary ever find true happiness?

Most experts believe it increasingly unlikely. "The last time she appeared at Lourdes," confides one, "I could have sworn I spotted cellulite."

As told to
CRAIG BROWN

BLAIR REVEALS SOURCE

by Our Political Correspondent **Michael Whitewash**

THE PRIME MINISTER, following repeated demands for him to reveal the source of his information concerning weapons of mass destruction, named "a senior figure with a beard".

Pressed further, the Prime Minister admitted that he had several meetings with the man who told him in strict confidence that "everything he did was absolutely right".

Journalists were at first slow to identify the source, but the Prime Minister gave them a series of clues, saying his name began with 'G' ended with 'D' and had an 'O' in the middle. Blair also explained that he lived on a cloud in the sky.

Heaven Eleven

A spokesman for God, however, denied that he was the source and suggested that the more likely source might be another bearded man with horns on his head and cloven hooves.

(Reuters)

'WE MAY NEVER FIND THE BLAME' – Blair Latest

by Our Defence Staff **W.M. Deedes**

AN UNREPENTANT Tony Blair admitted last night that the blame for Doctor Kelly's death "may never be found".

However, he told journalists that "this should not stop us pointing the finger at the BBC for the tragedy and believing that we were justified in launching a full-scale attack on them in the first place".

"He's been named by the BBC"

"Get me a spin-coroner!"

Exclusive to all Newspapers

Sad Day For Us All

DEATH of Dr Kelly... terrible tragedy... decent man... we are all to blame... blood on hands... moment of reflection... media excesses... dark forces... culture of dishonesty... a tragedy waiting to happen... step back to consider... judicial enquiry... truth must be told... fall guy... serious questions... one thing is for sure... nothing will ever be the same again...

© *All papers.*

TV: What You Missed
MY PILGRIMAGE
with **Brian R. Sewell**

(White-haired art historian seen driving ancient Mercedes along the North Circular)

Sewell *(for it is he)*: To be truthful I have no idea why I, at the age of 73, should be sitting here in a ten-mile tailback somewhere on the North Circular.

(Shot of cars standing still in heavy rain)

For hundreds of years pilgrims travelled along this very route that leads eventually to the heart of Neasden, known to the Romans as Neasdonia, and later a place of pilgrimage to the burial site of St Bruno, the patron saint of smoking – of which, alas, nothing remains today. I wonder: who are my fellow pilgrims on this long and infinitely tedious journey?

(Shot of interior of Ken's Cafe [Exit 94]. Sewell seen toying with the Ken's All-Day Special [egg, bacon, beans, sausage, chips, tomato, fried bread and cup of tea])

Sewell *(to cabbie)*: May I ask where you have come from?

Cabbie: Braintree in Essex is my domicile. But I was actually born in Wanstead.

Sewell: Wanstead? It sounds delightful!

(Overhead shot of Sewell's car taking wrong turning. Signpost points to "World Of Leather")

Sewell *(in car)*: This surely is a mistake. But nevertheless the World Of Leather does sound appealing. I wonder what I shall find...

(Cut to interior of large furniture showroom, full of leather sofas)

Salesman: This is our Florida range, Sir. It's fully upholstered, it comes in Deep Burgundy or Midnight Blue with the two matching chairs. We discount this range at £3,999 (delivery extra).

Sewell *(clutching umbrella)*: How perfectly hideous! *(Looks at camera)* It's hard to imagine the mentality of someone who could conceive of having such an utterly grotesque artefact in his home.

(Cut to Neasden football ground)

Sewell: At last, journey's end. But not a sign of St Bruno, let alone the famous Abbey which stood upon this spot. May I ask you good people whether you have come to pay your respects to this great spiritual leader of the Middle Ages?

Sid and Doris Bonkers *(for it is they)*: No, Squire, we 'ave come 'ere for the game.

Sewell: The game? What manner of game, may I ask? I see no pheasants.

Sid: No. Football match, mate. Dollis Hill.

Sewell: Football! How exhilarating! We see here this huge open space full of enthusiasm and excitement. This magnificent stadium, built, I believe, in 1941 by Prendergast and Crook...

(Shot of game in progress)

Sewell *(with Sid and Doris, waving scarves)*: We are indeed the pilgrims of today, with today's new religion. Surely if Giotto had been alive in our century he would have painted this very scene. The brightly coloured shirts. The thrills and spills...

(Neasden player sent off)

Sewell *(waving umbrella)*: The referee's a bastard!

Sid & Doris: Go on, you tell 'im, Brian!

(Music)

NEXT WEEK: *Brian Sewell continues his journey, trying to find an exit off the North Circular.*

ITV REFUSE TO REHIRE JOHN LESLIE

Apparently 'no' does mean 'no'

ULRIKA 'ASKED FOR IT'

by Our Showbiz Staff
Matthew Wrong

JOHN LESLIE has spoken about how he and Ulrika Jonsson enjoyed rampant publicity together from the first time they met.

"From the first moment we laid eyes on each other we both knew the only thing we wanted was to enjoy red hot publicity with each other," Leslie told reporters. "She was fantastic between the sheets of the tabloids and she told me afterwards that it was the best publicity she'd ever had."

Ulrika, however *(cont. p. 94)*

GEORGE PIST

The *Mail On Sunday*'s top columnist inexplicably writes every week in the *Mail*'s Night and Day Magazine.

The United States' Decision To Intervene In Liberia

● **What's your** problem, pal? You looking at me, you bastard? ... I love you... you're my best friend...

Lessons To Be Learned From The Kelly Inquiry

● **I tell you** something... I tell you something... I don't need a drink... I can handle it... Make that a double, barman... where am I?

Is The Novel Dead? Thoughts On The Booker Prize

● **I belong to** Glasgae... dear old... Shut yer face, yer bastard... do you know who I am?... Nor do I?

© Drunk Night And Day, The-Mail-On-Shunday-Or-Is-It-Thursday-I-Don't-Know

BUM COMES OUT AS BRITAIN SIZZLES!

by Our News Staff
Hugh Wottagh-Schorcher

80-90-100°! And still temperatures soared yesterday as British males boiled over at the sight of Kylie's bum.

Said one bum-baked Brit, "I don't know how I'm going to last the week. The bum is really hot and my brain has melted."

Pix 2, 3, 4, 5, 6, 7.
©*The Daily Telegraph*

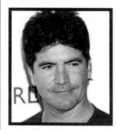

THOSE AMAZING SIMON COWELL PUT-DOWNS IN FULL

YES, he's back! The wittiest, rudest man on TV. Pop Idol's Mr Nasty is on our screens again with his acid tongue and his withering comments on the hopeful pop wannabees.

Here they are, a selection of Simon's vituperative verbal volleys!

■ *(To sad boy)*
"You're not a very good singer, are you?"

■ *(To sad girl)*
"You're not a very good singer either."

■ *(To next sad boy)*
"Your voice is worse than someone who isn't a very good singer."

■ *(To next sad girl)*
"Your voice makes the other not very good singer look like a good singer, which she isn't."

And, rudest of all, Simon's offensive dismissal that had Tracy Nargs in tears after she sang a cover version of Kylie Minogue's *Can't Get Your Bum Out Of My Head*:

Simon: *Well, Tracy, you're almost as talentless as me.*
© *All newspapers.*

"Have you had that lip treatment?"

Heatwave Round-Up
80-90-100!
by **Phil Space**

YES, IT'S official. Britain yesterday experienced a record number of pieces about how hot it is. The highest recorded number of articles was in the Daily Mail at exactly 101 (the most this century). It was closely followed by the Daily Telegraph (100.5), the Sun (99) and the Daily Mirror (98.4). The lowest recorded figure was in the Guardian with a mere 56.8 pieces (including an in-depth analysis of how all the other papers were covering the heatwave).

Said one holidaymaker, enjoying the articles in Great Yarmouth, "It's almost unbearable. I like pictures of semi-naked girls in fountains as much as the next man, but I'm not sure I can take it any longer."

And the Press Complaints Authority warned, "There's more to come".

80-90-100!
by **Phillipa Column**

YES, IT'S official. 100% of 'A' Level candidates in Britain have now passed the exam with flying colours. The highest recorded figure was in St Paul's Girls School in North London where the pass rate reached an astonishing 111% and even girls who didn't take the exam have scored A* in all subjects. And the government warned, "There's more to come".

80-90-100!
by **Phil Tufnell**

YES, IT'S official. The England cricket team has broken all the records, scoring 100 in a single innings.

And the English Cricket Board warned, "There's no more to come".

80-90-100!
by **Phil Paper**

YES, IT'S official. Bill Deedes has broken all the records by writing about the weather at the age of 100 and *(That's enough. Ed.)*

NEW CURE FOR COUGH FOUND

by Sir Thomas Beecham-Powder

SOME of Britain's top makeover specialists have been working round the clock to transform the leader of the opposition, Mr Iain Duncan Cough.

Every detail of the way he talks and walks has been changed, after feeding 10,000 details of Mr Cough's appearance and mannerisms into a computer.

The result, as can be seen below, is an astonishing transformation.

Gone is the dim, anonymous-looking, bald man with a cough who, for months, has won the lowest poll ratings in the history of the Conservative Party.

Now the former IDS will be projected to voters as 'SID', an attractive, bald man, with an engaging cough, and the benefit of not being over-exposed in the media.

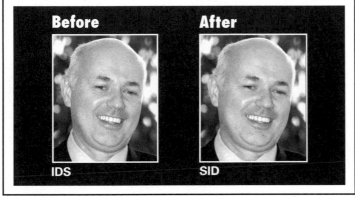

Before **IDS** After **SID**

BLAIR GOVERNMENT MILESTONE

by Clement Attlee

TONY BLAIR's government was celebrating a historic milestone this weekend as it broke the record for the number of consecutive days in office that a Labour government hadn't located weapons of mass destruction.

"This truly is an historic event that we do not want highlighted in any way at all," said the Prime (cont. p. 94)

GOVERNMENT SPOKESMAN APOLOGISES FOR KELLY SMEAR

I meant to say Walter Matthau

Film of the Week
NOW ON DVD

Monsieur Hoon's Holiday

Classic Film Comedy

■ Nothing goes right for the gangly Monsieur Hoon as he sets off for his annual holiday. No sooner has he left home than his world falls apart as his boss tries to sack him and everybody calls him a bastard. Hilarious sequence as he tries to set fire to an incriminating bag of secret papers and ends up getting his own fingers burnt.

108 minutes. Black and white. English subtitles.

S.GRIPE PAWNBROKER
KILMAN DISTILLERS
BABY NOT ON BAWD
with apologies to W. Hogarth

THAT NEW-LOOK DAILY TELEGRAPH DUMBED-DOWN CROSSWORD
(designed by the marketing department to attract younger and more stupid readers)

Across
1. Hugh Grant's former girlfriend, famous actress) (3,6).
Down
1. Famous actress, Hugh Grant's former girlfriend (3,6).

First correct answer wins free pin-up Daily Telegraph poster of Liz Hurley, signed by editor Charles Moore.

COMING SOON IN THE EYE

Cristina Odone writes on the joy of producing an article about childbirth.

'It was a long and painful process but it was worth it in the end – to hold in my arms a beautiful 500 pound cheque.'

A 'Gnometrash' article

C OF E SAYS 'SIN CAN BE WONDERFUL'

by Our Religious Staff **Lunchtime O'Done**

THE Church of England took another step into the 21st Century today when it published a new report entitled *Time To Be Open-Minded About Everything*.

The report, compiled by a number of bishops, argues that the time has come for the Church to move on from its old obsession with the "archaic and obsolete" idea of sin.

What Sin It For Me?

"To young people today," say the bishops, "the whole notion of sin is outside their frame of reference.

"When they are told that Christ died to save the world from sin they just stare in incomprehension."

The bishops argue that activities regarded in past ages as socially unacceptable – the so-called 'Seven Deadly Sins' – can now be seen to be life-enhancing expressions of the right of each individual to form their own value system in responding to the strains inseparable from living in modern society.

"Over the centuries," they say, "a whole lexicon of pejorative language has been developed to demonise certain perfectly healthy human instincts, such as sexuality, or the legitimate expression of righteous anger directed at a partner or colleague."

HOW THE BISHOPS HAVE REDEFINED 'SIN'

LUST: A natural expression of a human instinct common to all personkind.

SLOTH: A perfectly natural expression of the basic human right to reject oppressive societal nouns embodied in the so-called "work ethic".

GLUTTONY: One of the most encouraging developments of recent years has been the much greater appreciation of food and drink, thanks to the influence of such TV chefs as Jamie Oliver and Nigella Lawson. A modern, outward-looking Church should welcome this.

ENVY: It is a mark of how out of touch the Church has been in past ages that it was prepared to demonise the healthy human instinct to wish to share in the benefits enjoyed by better-off members of society.

(That's enough life-enhacing sins. Archbishop Rowan Pelling of the First Church of Christ Sensualist.)

LORD'S TEST

Who is out?

I am – and you should be in

News In Brief

IDS TO BE MADE AVAILABLE TO ALL

THE Labour Party has announced controversial plans to make IDS freely available to everyone.

"At present it's a real postcode lottery, with IDS being readily taken up by couples in their mid-50s in the home counties, but virtually nowhere else in the country," said a Labour spokesman, "and we aim to rectify that.

"Every day we are doing all we can to make sure that IDS is available to all as the next Prime Minister come the next election."

DA VINCI PAINTING – POLICE TO ACT

THE THEFT of the "Madonna with the Yarnwinder" has prompted the police to act quickly, it was revealed today.

"Once we heard of the nature of the painting, we immediately sprang into action," said a police spokesman, "and contacted our celebrity pervert squad to investigate Mr Da Vinci and ask him why he seems so keen to paint pictures of naked kiddies.

"From our sources, we understand he has fled to sixteenth-century Italy, so he must be guilty.

"The boys are very excited. This could be bigger than Matthew Kelly."

Those Dangerous Diets In Full

The Atkinson Diet

NON-STOP diet of Mr Bean, can cause extreme weariness and lethargy, particularly on short-haul flights at this time of year.

The Anne Atkins Diet

NON-STOP diet of silly agony aunt pieces in the Daily Telegraph, can cause immediate irritation and nausea.

The Aitken Diet

NON-STOP diet of prison food, leads to dramatic loss of weight and the shedding of millions of pounds.

The Nutkin Diet

NON-STOP diet of high protein nuts, can lead to development of bushy tail and a tendency to tree dwelling.

The Nutcase Diet

NON-STOP diet of steak, bacon and eggs, can cause death by boredom in those having to read about it endlessly in the newspapers.

"I'm on the Tommy Atkins diet – muck and bullets"

THE BOOK OF SHARON

Chapter 94

1. And lo, it came to pass that Sharon decreed that a mighty wall should be raised betwixt the lands of the children of Israel and the land of the Arab-ites.

2. And Sharon said: "Let the wall be fourteen cubits high and six cubits thick, so that no Arab-ites or Hamas-ites or Hezboll-ites may ever again cross over into the land of Israel."

3. For Sharon had wearied of the troubles that had been brought upon the children of Israel by the Hamas-ites and the Hezboll-ites and all the other -ites, when they came privily unto the land of Israel and slew both themselves and the Israelites, like even unto Samson.

4. Then did the Israelites go forth to do Sharon's bidding and raise a mighty wall around all the land of the Arab-ites.

5. And they separated fathers and mothers from their children, brother from brother, sister from sister.

6. And the houses of the Arab-ites were left without water to drink nor soil to be tilled.

7. And the orange groves and olive trees were laid waste, and there was much wailing and gnashing of teeth.

8. And the Arab-ites said, one to another: "Woe is us, for this wall of Sharon has made our homes a prison and our land no more than a barren wilderness, where there is no sound in the noonday save the roaring of the bull that is called dozer."

9. But Sharon looked upon his wall and saw that it was good.

10. And to the wailing of the Arab-ites and their women and children, Sharon hardened his heart, saying: "Verily, that which they have asked for, that they have got."

11. Then Sharon journeyed unto the land of Us, even unto the House that is called White, where dwelleth the ruler of that land that is called Dub-ya.

12. And Dub-ya saith unto Sharon: "Behold, I have seen a vision that I am the man, sent by God, to bring peace, that shall be forever between your people and the peoples of the Arab-ites, even the Hamas-ites, the Hezboll-ites and the rest of the -ites that are too numerous to mention."

13. And Dub-ya said unto Sharon: "To this end have I called thee, that thou shouldst give the word that this wall thou hast built must be taken down, brick by brick, so that once again the Arab-ites can go forth into their fields and draw water and eat of the fruit of the pomegranate tree whose seed they have planted and which has borne fruit by their labours, even an hundredfold."

14. And Sharon listened unto Dub-ya with a face that is straight, until Dub-ya had come to the last word of his utterance.

15. And Sharon saith unto him: "I hear what thou sayest, O mighty ruler of Us, but the answer from the children of Israel is that thou must be joking."

16. And so it was that the children of Israel proceeded with the building of the wall of Sharon, even until every last brick of it was in place.

17. And the Arab-ites looked upon Sharon's wall and wept bitterly, for they knew that it would bright them naught but suffering and grief.

18. And the Arab-ites and the Hamas-ites and and Hezboll-ites took counsel among themselves and said: "Let us now rise up privily and discover some new way in which we can seek vengeance on the children of Israel."

19. And so it was that they came back to the square that is called one.

(Here doth not end the lesson that is not learned)

From the Board of Directors of British Jews

Dear Sir,

We have read with outrage the above chapter of the Bible. A clearer example of anti-Semitism it would be hard to find outside the pages of Der Sturmer. We demand that all copies of this deeply offensive book be withdrawn from sale herewith.

Yours,
RABBI AMIEL OF CROSSHARBOUR,
c/o The Daily Telegraph

MARS: WHAT YOU CAN SEE

Canals

Deserts

Mountain ranges

Weapons of mass destruction

"She hasn't been quite the same since she posed for our fundraising calendar"

Times

IS IT TIME FOR LIAR GILLIGAN TO COMMIT SUICIDE?

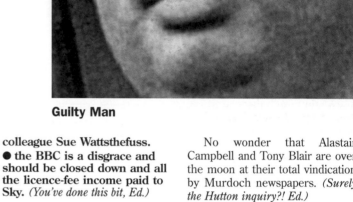

Guilty Man

By **Trevor Grovellagh**

AFTER only one day of the Hutton inquiry, one thing is clear.

The BBC must be closed down immediately and all the licence-fee income given to Sky.

Yesterday, under relentless cross-examination, the fat, sweaty toad Gilligan finally broke down and admitted the following:
- his story was correct.
- it was corroborated by his colleague Sue Wattsthefuss.
- the BBC is a disgrace and should be closed down and all the licence-fee income paid to Sky. *(You've done this bit, Ed.)*

There's More Of This In The Sun!

No wonder that Alastair Campbell and Tony Blair are over the moon at their total vindication by Murdoch newspapers. *(Surely the Hutton inquiry?! Ed.)*

Surely it cannot be long now before those weapons of mass destruction turn up in Mr Gilligan's bedroom? *Full story: pages 2-16.*

THE TIMES FRIDAY AUGUST 8 2003

Kelly's links to Al Qaeda

by Our Political Staff Tom Baldlie

THE disgraced former Ministry of Defence scientist Dr David Kelly may have been connected to the terrorist group Al Qaeda, writes **Alastair Campbell** *(surely "Times Top Political Staff? Ed.)*

Sources close to Osama bin Laden claim that Dr Kelly's religion, the fundamentalist semi-muslim sect of Bali Hi, was actually a cover for the terrorist group, although there is no evidence at all to substantiate this claim, since it is obviously true. Particularly since Dr Kelly, although happily married with children, was known to have a number of gay friends, many of whom he will have met as an outpatient at the Priory where he may well have been undergoing treatment for a lifelong addiction to alcohol, narcotics and of course depression, which could well have led him to take his own life rather than anything which the government may or may not have done.

The Enquiry, led by Lord Sitton, will have to consider all these facts about Kelly being bonkers before coming to its conclusion that Alastair Campbell and Mr Blair are clear of any blame whatsoever.

On other pages

'Turn off your BBC' says our Media Editor **Rupert Murdoch**.

"Helluva half-time team talk"

HUTTON INQUIRY – DAY 94

AS LORD Hutton's inquiry into the events surrounding the death of Dr David Kelly, the government scientist at the heart of the *(We know all this – get on with it. Ed.)*

The inquiry yesterday heard the evidence of a Ministry of Defence official, Mr Kevin Paperclip, who was in charge of interdepartmental liaison between the Joint Defence Intelligence Committee (JDIC) and the department's Strategic Intelligence Assessment Unit (SIAU).

Answering questions from Mr Andrew Earnalot Q.C., Mr Paperclip said he had no direct knowledge of the so-called "sexed up" dossier, but he had been briefed on "more than one occasion" by the head of the Defence Intelligence Co-ordination Committee (DICC).

Earnalot: Was it, or was it not, your impression, Mr Paperclip, that the second dossier had been rewritten following the meeting on 24 January on which we heard evidence yesterday.

Paperclip: It may well have been. I cannot honestly recall.

Hugefee: Are you seriously

A dramatic moment during the evidence of Keith Filingcabinet

expecting this inquiry to believe that you cannot remember?

Paperclip: I have accessed my 'palm-top' diary for the day in question, but the only data I have been able to retrieve was an urgent memorandum from Mrs Paperclip reminding me to purchase three tins of Whiskas on my way home.

Lord Hutton: We have heard a good deal about this 'palm-top' device, Mr Earnalot.

Could you perhaps enlighten us as to what this term refers to?

Earnalot: I understand, m'lud, that it is a type of cat food.

Huttoncarrot: I am indebted to you.

(The inquiry continues)

The Memo That Rocked the BBC

AMONG yesterday's witnesses was Mr Sam Brook, the Deputy Head of the BBC Bi-Medial News and Current Affairs Analysis Unit, who told Lord Hutton that, on 24 May, he had sent a memo to the Assistant Chief of the Newsgathering (Politics) Liaison Group, drawing attention to the internal memo by Miss Susan Wattsthestory to the Executive Producer of Newsnight (Science and Current Affairs) asking for clarification of the guidelines relating to 'the use of dictaphone machines in an evidential context'.

The inquiry heard that the e-mail reply to Ms Wattsitallabout had been lost due to an administrative error.

The Wattsit Tape In Full

Sue Watts: Hullo, Dr Kelly? Did you hear the Today programme yesterday?

Kelly: Hi, Sue, I certainly did and I might have a bit of a story for you on that.

Watts: Really?

Kelly: Yes, apparently this dossier, it was sexed-up a bit, probably by this Campbell chap at Number 10.

Watts: No, I don't think so. But thanks for letting me know. I've got to go now to pick up some cat food before the shops shut.

Hutton – The Timetable of Terror

FOR THE first time, the inquiry yesterday managed to pin down the exact sequence of events which led up to the accusation that Alastair Campbell had asked for a redrafting of the memorandum which related to the inclusion in the dossier of 14 January a reference to "45 minutes" as the time it would take Mr Paperclip to pick up a tin of Whiskas on his way home from Whitehall to 147 Valerie Grove, Blackheath.

2.36 pm Mohammed Nodes, a retail display manager employed by the New Cross branch of Londis, restacks shelves in the pet food department with tins of Whiskas.

3.15 pm Mr Paperclip leaves War Office to catch No. 12 bus.

(That's enough 'Timetable of Terror'. Ed.)

MAN NOT CALLED KELLY FOUND DEAD – NO INQUIRY HELD

A BRITISH soldier was today found dead in Iraq, the 50th casualty of the decision to invade *(Contd. p. 94)*

Egyptian Rhyming Slang

BRITAIN'S TOP SUPER-SPY EMERGES FROM THE SHADOWS

by Top Sketchwriter
Quentin Lettspretendthisisinteresting

THE HUTTON Inquiry came alive yesterday, when the mystery figure of Britain's legendary cloak-and-dagger spy chief, known only as John Scarlett (*surely 'H'? Ed.*), emerged blinking from the murky, shadowy world of John Le Carré's Smiley into the harsh spotlight of Court 97.

Reporters gasped with amazement as they at last saw for the first time a figure so mysterious that many of them doubted he even existed.

Suddenly, there he was – a small, bald, bespectacled man in a suit.

Could this really be the legendary 'X', a spy so brilliant that he was once expelled from Moscow for going up to Mr Brezhnev with a copy of the Times under his arm and asking, "Have you got any secrets you'd like to tell me? I'm from British Intelligence. Very hush-hush, you know"?

Certainly, the super-spy lived up to his billing, as he faced a ruthless two-hour grilling from one of Britain's most highly-paid QCs, Mr James Dingieperson.

It was an incredible, bravura tour-de-force which no one who saw it will ever remember.

That Scarlett Cross-Examination In Full

Sir Huge Dingiedrawers QC: Mr Scarlett, was any pressure put on you to 'sex up' the dossier in question?

Scarface: No.

Dingiepants: What about this e-mail from your friend Mr Campbell reading "Come on, Scarlett, you'll need to do better than this if we're going to send a million men to their deaths." Did you consider this memo to be in any way putting pressure on you to amend the dossier in a way that Mr Campbell would have found more conducive to his case?

Scarlatti: No.

Dingieknickers: Did or did you not, Mr Scarlett, alter the wording of the dossier from "there is a faint possibility that Mr Hussein might possibly have the ability to develop nuclear weapons within 45 years, but we can't be sure" to "we're all going to die in 45 minutes"?

Sir Gerald Scarfe: No.

Dingietrunks: But that is what happened, is it not, to the wording of the dossier?

Scarbootsale: It was not a dossier. It was a document designed to provide a background intelligence assessment on a matter of sensitivity pertaining to Mr Campbell's desire for the public to be fully informed on all matters relating to Iraq.

Dingiepoos: Please answer "no" or "no".

Scarlett O'Hara: No.

Dingiehose: Are you aware of this email marked "Top Secret – For Your Eyes Only", which was sent you yesterday morning from someone calling himself 'C'? It says, "If they start asking you about the dossier, just say 'no' to everything, okay? See you for dinner later."

Scarlet Pimpernel: No.

Rubberdinghy: Is there anything you would like to add?

Scartissue: No.

The Inquiry continues.

HOON ROCKS INQUIRY

IN AN electrifying performance, Defence Secretary Geoff Hoon, widely billed as the "fall guy" for the Government's "sexed-up dossier" fiasco, defied expectations by telling the inquiry that he could not remember if he knew anything about the events which had led up to whatever it was that had happened.

Asked if he had been responsible for the naming of Dr Kelly, Hoon replied, "Who is Dr Kelly? I am sorry that I have no idea who he is."

When asked whether he had had any contact with the prime minister, Hoon sipped from a glass of water before replying, "I am not sure who you are referring to. In any case, that would be something that would be dealt with by my officials."

When pressed by Mr Dinjaturtle QC as to what exactly he did do, Mr Hoon said, "It is not up to me to define the parameters of what I do. You will have to put that question to someone from Number 10."

Lord Hutton finally intervened to ask Mr Hoon whether he knew anything about anything at all. "I have no idea," replied the Defence Secretary, "I was on holiday at the time."

CAPTAIN SCARLETT IN MYSTERON INQUIRY

by Our Political Correspondent
Gerry Bruce Anderson

Dateline Earth 2003

TOP SECRET agent **Captain Scarlett was today accused of overstating the threat of the Mysterons.**

Scarlett, one of the senior figures in the intelligence agency Spectrum, was responsible for a document claiming that the so-called Mysterons had established a base on Venus from which they could launch an attack on earth "within 45 minutes".

Scarlett further claimed that the

Mysterons had developed Weapons of Mars Destruction from their home planet and were planning to destroy the entire world.

Colonel Whitewash

Scarlett explained to the Inquiry that he had relied on a single Mysteron source who had told him, "This is the voice of the Mysterons" – as a result of which he had decided to invade the universe.

Captain Conrad Black is 79.

● Tomorrow: *Doctor Hoon and the Daleks.*

Nursery Times

Friday, 5 September, 2003

'YES, I KILLED COCK ROBIN,' ADMITS SPARROW

by Our Ornithological Staff **John Bird**

THE INQUIRY into the death of Cock Robin was rocked yesterday by the dramatic admission by the Sparrow that he "bore the ultimate responsibility for the sad death of Cock Robin".

Lord Owl, who has been hearing evidence from witnesses such as the Fly and the Fish, asked Cock Robin if he was admitting to the crime.

"I am responsible," said the Sparrow, "although it was of course entirely the fault of Cock Robin himself."

THE TIMES FRIDAY SEPTEMBER 5 2003

The Prime Minister's Historic Evidence

The appearance of Mr Blair at the Hutton Inquiry last week banished any lingering doubts about his conduct in the unfortunate death of Dr Kelly at the hands of the BBC.

His statesmanlike performance... supremely confident... mastery of facts... critics rebuffed... on top of his brief... extremely professional... sober delivery... absence of spin... contrast to BBC chairman... shifty demeanour... weasel words... silly beard... born liar if ever we saw one... licence-payers' money... time to close down the BBC... watch Sky TV... hoorah for Mr Murdoch.

© *The Sun.*

ON OTHER PAGES 'It's all going well in Iraq' writes Tim Hamas **2** 'Bush will be re-elected by a landslide' writes Michael Gofer **3** 'My daughter says politics is like the dodgems' by Mary Ann Bighead *(as seen on TV).*

Those Planned Sweeping Reforms To BBC News In The Wake Of The Hutton Inquiry In Full

1. News department to be merged with Downing Street Press Office.

2. Tony Blair to replace Huw Edwards as host of 10 O'Clock News.

3. Er...

4. That's it.

"That one!"

RAT TO LEAVE SINKING SHIP

by Our Shipping Staff **Joshua Rodentberg**

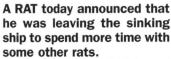

A RAT today announced that he was leaving the sinking ship to spend more time with some other rats.

"I have been thinking of leaving the ship for a long time and I have discussed it at length with the captain." said the rat. "The fact that the ship is going down has not influenced my decision at all."

Alastair Campbell

In a letter to the captain the rat says, "It has been a privilege to be on this ship for all these years and to serve you in my capacity as a rat."

The captain in turn thanked the rat for his loyal service and described him as "a great friend, a great colleague and a great rat."

Alastair Campbell

Rat experts were quick to praise the rat's contribution to the sinking of the ship (*Surely "successful voyage of the vessel"? Ed.)* Said Roy Greentail, "I used to work with the rat in the old days in the gutter. He was a good rat to have on your side. He was rough, tough, with a thick skin and a long dirty tale which no-one believed."

Alastair Campbell

Another former colleague remembers the rat from their days on board Captain Bob's ill-fated vessel.

"He was a prize example of vermin. I once got into a scrap with him when he turned nasty and bit me on the nose. He was responsible for the Black Death and the Plague but apart from that he was a decent, honest, straightforward sort of rat."

The rat pledged his loyalty to the captain saying he would be available for consultancy "but only from the safety of the shore."

BAGHDAD TIMES

Friday September 5 2003

POST-WAR CHAOS
Power Failures Continue

by Our Man In London **Sir John Keegan**

THE CAPITAL city of this once-proud country was plunged into hours of terrifying darkness as a result of the authorities' failure to maintain electricity supplies.

Frightened Londoners were trapped in nightmare conditions as lights went out, trains ground to a halt and hospitals were forced to resort to emergency generators.

Millions of civilians staggered around in the dark, not knowing when the lights would come on again.

"The irony," said one furious Londoner, "is that this country has all that North Sea oil, yet we can't get the lights to come on so that we can eat our tea."

NO SHOCK
(because electricity was off)

He continued, "Mr Bush's man, who is supposed to be in charge here, is failing utterly in his job."

Meanwhile, extremists have taken advantage of the chaotic conditions for their own political advantage.

The self-styled leader of Britain's three million newt-lovers, Ayatollah Red Ken, has urged people to protest: "Once again, we see a lack of investment in the infrastructure of our public services," he screamed.

"Imagine the situation if this had happened during the heatwave – millions would have died. It is time to get rid of Blair and appoint a Prime Minister who has the support of local people, such as myself."

93

CAN READING THE MAIL GIVE YOU CANCER?

By Our Medical Staff **Dr Atkins**

A NEW study has shown a definite link between reading the Daily Mail and getting cancer.

Scientists now believe that the Mail is an active carcinogen, raising levels of stress and worry among its readers to such a point that they trigger the growth of cancerous cells.

Dangerous Rubbish

Writing in the prestigious medical journal *Scares and Scaremongers*, Dr Hackenbusch of the University of New Rothermere claims that four out of every 10 people who regularly read the Daily Mail will die of cancer.

What happens is that the typical reader begins by worrying about dieting and health problems, then progresses to chronic anxiety induced by reading articles about rising crime and illegal immigrants.

The reader finally succumbs to suicidal depression triggered by yet another forecast of house prices.

Hysterical Lies

At this point, the Mail reader's immune system breaks down, and he or she soon sinks into a coma which can only end in death.

BUSH PLEDGES NEW WAR ON TERROR

by Our U.N. Staff **W.M. Deedes**

IN A shock speech to the United Nations, U.S. President Bush claimed that Iraq was now a hotbed of terrorism.

"The world must act," he said, "to stamp out this evil cancer of terrorism which is threatening to destabilise the entire Middle East region.

"It is now clear," he went on, "that the forces of Mr Saddam and his friend Al Q'aeda have joined up, just as I always predicted they would.

"There is only one way we can rid the world of this threat. We must invade Iraq at once."

Mr Bush's call was immediately supported by the British prime minister. "I have given orders," he said, "that all surviving British forces must withdraw from Iraq, so that we can re-invade at once."

STOP PRESS

Opposition Leader Tipped To Restore Order To Iraq

THE U.S. occupation forces are believed to favour the return of the controversial Iraqi leader Saddam Hussein, as the only man who can bring peace to terror-torn Iraq *(Reuters)*

Why Tories Will Win

by The World's Worst Columnist **Sir Hitler Hastings**

AT LAST I believe the Tory leader Iain Duncan Cough has found the secret weapon which will guarantee his victory by a landslide at the next election.

I refer of course to his pledge, revealed exclusively in the current issue of *Fish and Fishermen*, that the next Conservative government will abolish the most iniquitous and hated legislative burden ever imposed on the British people – namely the 5/- a year fishing licence.

Magna Carta

To those of us who realise that the most pleasurable pastime known to man is to stand by the bank of the Itchen or the Test, holding in one's hand a £2000 cheque from the *Daily Mail (Surely 'Hurley and Paltrow fishing rod'? Ed.)*, whiling away an innocent few hours in pursuit of Johnny Trout or Jack Salmon *(Keep going. Ed.)*.

With unerring political acumen, Iain Duncan Cough has placed his finger on the one issue that unites every true-born Englishman.

I remember when I was a boy, my father taking me to the river bank and throwing me in. "Now, my boy," he called out, "you know what it feels like to be a fish."

It is a lesson I have never forgotten.

© Max Hitler 2003.

■ *If you would like to read more of Sir Max Hastings's articles for the Daily Mail, you must be mad.*

POETRY CORNER

In Memoriam
Bob Hope, Comedian

So. Farewell
Then
Finally
Bob Hope.

Comedian,
Film star
And very
Rich.

Keith's Mum says that
You won World War Two
By entertaining
The troops.

But other historians
Believe that is
Putting it
A bit
Strongly.

Still, now
You are on
"The Road
To Heaven".

E.J. Thribb (aged 117½)

In Memoriam
Charles Bronson

So. Farewell
Then
Charles Bronson.

Yes, you were
One of "The
Magnificent Seven".

Now, following
The deaths of Yul
Brynner, James
Coburn, Horst
Buchholtz, Steve
McQueen and the
Other one

There is only Robert
Vaughn left.

"The Magnificent One"
As he will
Now be known.

All together now –

Dum. Di-da-da-dum
Dum. Di-da-da-dum

Da-da
Di-da-DA-da...

E.J. Thribb (aged 17½)

95

**66 CHESTER SQUARE
LONDON W1**

Dear Bill,

I got a stiffy from the Telegraph last week inviting me to celebrate your 90th with a tincture or twain at the Travellers Club. Forgive me if I decline. Much as I would like to sink not one but several helpings of the electric soup in your honour, I have to tell you that since my recent brush with the Reaper (by-the-by please thank Daphne for sending those nasturtiums if that's what they were), I am under strict instructions from Dr O'Gooley to forswear the Demon Drink.

The other thing – strictly entre nous – is that I don't really like leaving the old girl on her own of an evening. I slipped out the other night to sip a Perrier with Boris (now working at MI5 cleaning the carpets) and when I got back I found her on the blower to that red-faced bruiser Ingham, telling him to call a press conference immediately and announce that Blair had asked her to fly out to Baghdad to head the interim government. The trouble is, Bill, she's got it into her head that little Blair is "one of us" and that the Tories are still in charge. "The Party is in good hands, Denis," she keeps saying, ignoring my repeated assertion that Blair represents the Smellysocks.

Quite honestly, Bill, I can't altogether blame her for the confusion. Blair may well be, in our eyes, the most frightful smarmy-voiced prat, but you have to hand it to him for cracking down on the Reds in his ranks. The one I heartily approve of is Brother Blunkett, telling the coons they'd better learn to speak English and bundling the asylum-seekers back to the Departure Lounge. More power to his elbow, say I (as does the

> **The Editor of
> The Daily Telegraph**
> invites you to celebrate
> **The 90th Birthday of W.F. Deedes**
> to be held in
> The Library, The Travellers Club, 106 Pall Mall, London SW1
> on Wednesday 28th May 2003
> RSVP: The Daily Telegraph

Major, who's got a pack of Albanians camping in his back garden down in Kent). Given this sensible approach to social problems, what's the point of the little bald pixie Duncan Smith? About as much use as a one-legged man at an arse-kicking contest, I'd say.

I have to admit I do admire you for soldiering on at the Telegraph. I had to go to Canary Wharf once to try and pacify some insurance brokers who were threatening to sue the Boy Mark for non-payment of the odd million. What a dump, Bill! Not a saloon bar in sight. Just crowds of yuppies wandering about in the shade of the skyscrapers talking into their mobiles or queuing for cappuccinos at £3.99 a go. I don't know how you stand it. As for that new boss of yours, Conrad Black, I had to sit next to him once at a dinner party in honour of that croaky-voiced German who used to run errands for Nixon (Basinger? Massingberd? No matter). What a crasher, Bill! He spent the whole evening droning on about Napoleon and even explained the Battle of Waterloo with a handful of fishknives and a salt-cellar. He's married to a little doll-faced creature who Boris tells me is a highly-paid Mossad agent.

A propos the Telegraph, do you ever come across a very strange-looking cove called Charles Moore, who claims to be a colleague of yours? Only he's writing the official life of the Boss in exchange for a six-figure sum and comes round here every so often with his notebook and sharpened pencil to take dictation. Perfectly well-spoken and nicely dressed but totally out of touch with the real world, rather like that poofy sky-pilot friend of Maurice's who was slung out of AA for serving whisky at the tea break. He sits there gazing up at the Boss with adoring eyes while she tells him how she got the better of Mitterrand by flooding the Channel Tunnel and other fanciful tales. Little Moore writes it all down in his book and obviously hasn't twigged that half the time she's away with the fairies.

The last time he was here he said as he took his leave that he hoped he'd see me at your 90th bash and that he "of course" would be saying a few words. I have to point out, Bill, that much as I love you the thought of a lot of sweaty Telegraph reptiles plus Brother Moore pontificating in plummy tones – the only comfort being a glass of iced Perrier with a slice of lemon – was enough to confirm my decision to stay well away.

Yours in the bed nearest the door,

Denis